Mastering Python Network Automation

Automating Container Orchestration, Configuration, and Networking with Terraform, Calico, HAProxy, and Istio

Tim Peters

Published by: GitforGits
Publisher: Sonal Dhandre
www.gitforgits.com
support@gitforgits.com

Printed in India

First Printing: March 2023

ISBN: 978-8196228552

Cover Design by: Kitten Publishing

Content

Preface

With "Mastering Python Network Automation," you can streamline container orchestration, configuration management, and resilient networking with Python and its libraries, allowing you to emerge as a skilled network engineer or a strong DevOps professional.

From the ground up, this guide walks readers through setting up a network automation lab using the NS3 network simulator and Python programming. This includes the installation of NS3, as well as python libraries like nornir, paramiko, netmiko, and PyEZ, as well as the configuration of ports, hosts, and servers. This book will teach you the skills to become a proficient automation developer who can test and fix any bugs in automation scripts. This book examines the emergence of the service mesh as a solution to the problems associated with service-to-service communication over time.

This book walks you through automating various container-related tasks in Python and its libraries, including container orchestration, service discovery, load balancing, container storage management, container performance monitoring, and rolling updates. Calico and Istio are two well-known service mesh tools, and you'll find out how to set them up and configure them to manage traffic routing, security, and monitoring.

Additional topics covered in this book include the automation of network policies, the routing of workloads, and the collection and monitoring of metrics, logs, and traces. You'll also pick up some tips and tricks for collecting and visualising Istio metrics with the help of tools like Grafana.

In this book you will learn how to:

- Use of Istio for cluster traffic management, traffic routing, and service mesh implementation.
- Utilizing Cilium and Calico to solve pod networking and automate network policy and workload routing.
- Monitoring and managing Kubernetes clusters with etcd and HAProxy load balancers and container storage.
- Establishing network automation lab with tools like NS3 emulator, Python, Virtual Environment, and VS Code.
- Establishing connectivity between hosts, port connectivity, SSH connectivity, python libraries, NS3, and network encryption.

GitforGits

Prerequisites

"Mastering Python Network Automation" is an essential guide for network engineers, DevOps professionals, and developers who want to streamline container orchestration and resilient networking with the help of Terraform, Calico, and Istio. Knowing Python and basics of networking is sufficient to pursue this book.

Codes Usage

Are you in need of some helpful code examples to assist you in your programming and documentation? Look no further! Our book offers a wealth of supplemental material, including code examples and exercises.

Not only is this book here to aid you in getting your job done, but you have our permission to use the example code in your programs and documentation. However, please note that if you are reproducing a significant portion of the code, we do require you to contact us for permission.

But don't worry, using several chunks of code from this book in your program or answering a question by citing our book and quoting example code does not require permission. But if you do choose to give credit, an attribution typically includes the title, author, publisher, and ISBN. For example, "Mastering Python Network Automation by Tim Peters".

If you are unsure whether your intended use of the code examples falls under fair use or the permissions outlined above, please do not hesitate to reach out to us at support@gitforgits.com.

We are happy to assist and clarify any concerns.

Acknowledgement

I owe a tremendous debt of gratitude to GitforGits, for their unflagging enthusiasm and wise counsel throughout the entire process of writing this book. Their knowledge and careful editing helped make sure the piece was useful for people of all reading levels and comprehension skills. In addition, I'd like to thank everyone involved in the publishing process for their efforts in making this book a reality. Their efforts, from copyediting to advertising, made the project what it is today.

Finally, I'd like to express my gratitude to everyone who has shown me unconditional love and encouragement throughout my life. Their support was crucial to the completion of this book. I appreciate your help with this endeavour and your continued interest in my career.

Chapter 1: Python Essentials for Networks

Role of Python in Network Programming

Overview

Python is a popular programming language that is widely used in the field of network programming and network automation. Python's popularity for network programming stems from its simplicity, flexibility, and extensive collection of libraries and frameworks that make it easy to work with network devices and protocols. This chapter explores the concept of Python's ease of use for network programming and network automation.

Python is an interpreted language that is easy to learn and use, making it a popular choice for network programmers and network engineers. Python's syntax is easy to read and understand, and the language provides a rich set of tools and libraries that simplify network programming tasks. For instance, Python's standard library includes modules for handling networking protocols such as TCP/IP, UDP, and HTTP, making it easier to work with these protocols in Python code.

Factors Benefitting Networking

One of the most popular libraries for network programming in Python is the Socket library. The Socket library provides an interface for creating network sockets, which are endpoints for network communication. With the Socket library, Python developers can create client-server applications, send and receive data over network connections, and handle network errors and exceptions.

Python's ease of use for network programming is also due to the availability of third-party libraries and frameworks. For instance, the Paramiko library is a popular Python library for working with Secure Shell (SSH) protocols. With Paramiko, Python developers can establish SSH connections with network devices, execute commands on remote devices, and transfer files over the network. Similarly, the Netmiko library is a Python library for working with network devices such as routers and switches. With Netmiko, Python developers can automate network device configuration, backup and restore network configurations, and collect device information.

Another reason why Python is popular for network automation is its integration with other tools and technologies. For example, Python can be used with Ansible, a popular IT automation tool, to automate network tasks such as device configuration and monitoring. Python can also be used with the Simple Network Management Protocol (SNMP) to monitor network devices, collect network statistics, and troubleshoot network issues.

To conclude, Python's ease of use for network programming and network automation stems from its simplicity, flexibility, and extensive collection of libraries and frameworks. Python provides an easy-to-learn syntax, a rich set of tools and libraries for network programming, and seamless integration with other tools and technologies. Python's popularity in the field of network programming and network automation is set to grow as more organizations adopt automation and seek to streamline their network operations.

Learn to use Data Types

Python is a dynamically typed language that supports several data types. A data type is a classification of data that determines the type of operations that can be performed on it. In this chapter, we will discuss the different data types supported by Python along with examples and illustrations.

Numeric Data Types

Python supports various numeric data types such as integers, floating-point numbers, and complex numbers.

Integers

An integer is a whole number, either positive or negative, without a decimal point. In Python, integers are represented by the int class. For example, 5, -10, and 0 are all integers.

```
x = 5
y = -10
print(x, y)
```

Output:

```
5 -10
```

Floating-Point Numbers

A floating-point number is a number that has a decimal point. In Python, floating-point numbers are represented by the float class. For example, 3.14 and -2.5 are floating-point numbers.

```
x = 3.14
y = -2.5
print(x, y)
```

Output:

```
3.14 -2.5
```

Complex Numbers

A complex number is a number that has both a real and imaginary part. In Python, complex numbers are represented by the complex class. For example, 3 + 4j is a complex number where 3 is the real part and 4j is the imaginary part.

```
x = 3 + 4j
y = -2 - 3j
print(x, y)
```

Output:

```
(3+4j) (-2-3j)
```

Boolean Data Type

A boolean data type is a data type that can have one of two possible values: True or False. In Python, boolean values are represented by the bool class. Boolean values are used in conditional statements and loops to control program flow.

```
x = True
y = False
print(x, y)
```

Output:

```
True False
```

Sequence Data Types

Python supports several sequence data types such as strings, lists, tuples, and range objects.

Strings

A string is a sequence of characters. In Python, strings are represented by the str class. Strings can be enclosed in single quotes ('...') or double quotes ("...") or triple quotes ('''...''' or """""...""""").

```
x = 'Hello'
```

```
y = "World"
print(x, y)
```

Output:

```
Hello World
```

Lists

A list is a collection of items that are ordered and changeable. In Python, lists are represented by the list class. Lists can contain any data type, including other lists.

```
x = [1, 2, 3, 'four', 5.5]
y = ['apple', 'banana', 'cherry']
print(x, y)
```

Output:

```
[1, 2, 3, 'four', 5.5] ['apple', 'banana', 'cherry']
```

Tuples

A tuple is a collection of items that are ordered and immutable. In Python, tuples are represented by the tuple class. Tuples can contain any data type, including other tuples.

```
x = (1, 2, 3, 'four', 5.5)
y = ('apple', 'banana', 'cherry')
print(x, y)
```

Output:

```
(1, 2, 3, 'four', 5.5) ('apple', 'banana', 'cherry')
```

Range Objects

A range object is an immutable sequence of numbers. In Python, range objects are created using the range() function. Range objects are commonly used in loops to execute a set of instructions a certain number of times.

```
x = range(0, 10)
for i in x:
    print(i)
```

Output:

```
0
1
2
3
4
5
6
7
8
9
```

Mapping Data Types

Python supports a mapping data type called a dictionary.

Dictionaries

A dictionary is an unordered collection of key-value pairs. In Python, dictionaries are represented by the dict class. Dictionaries are used to store and retrieve data based on a key rather than an index.

```
x = {'name': 'John', 'age': 25, 'city': 'New York'}
y = {1: 'one', 2: 'two', 3: 'three'}
print(x, y)
```

Output:

```
{'name': 'John', 'age': 25, 'city': 'New York'} {1: 'one', 2: 'two', 3: 'three'}
```

Set Data Types

Python supports a set data type.

Sets

A set is an unordered collection of unique elements. In Python, sets are represented by the set class. Sets are used to perform mathematical set operations such as union, intersection, and difference.

```
x = {1, 2, 3, 4, 5}
y = {4, 5, 6, 7, 8}
print(x, y)
```

Output:

```
{1, 2, 3, 4, 5} {4, 5, 6, 7, 8}
```

Binary Data Types

Python supports two binary data types, bytes and bytearray.

Bytes

A bytes object is an immutable sequence of bytes. In Python, bytes objects are represented by the bytes class.

```
x = b'Hello'
y = b'\x48\x65\x6c\x6c\x6f'
print(x, y)
```

Output:

```
b'Hello' b'Hello'
```

Bytearray

A bytearray object is a mutable sequence of bytes. In Python, bytearray objects are represented by the bytearray class.

```
x = bytearray(b'Hello')
x[0] = 72
print(x)
```

Output:

```
bytearray(b'Hello')
```

Overall, Python supports various data types such as numeric, boolean, sequence, mapping, set, and binary data types. Understanding these data types and their characteristics is essential to write efficient and effective Python programs.

Exploring Loops

Loops in Python are used to execute a set of instructions repeatedly. There are two types of loops in Python: for loops and while loops. In this tutorial, we will discuss both types of loops with practical examples.

For Loops

For loops are used to iterate over a sequence (such as a list, tuple, or string) or other iterable objects (such as a dictionary or a file). The syntax of the for loop is as follows:

```
for variable in sequence:
    # Code to be executed
```

The for loop first initializes the variable with the first value in the sequence. Then, it executes the code block until the last value in the sequence is reached.

Example#1: Looping through a list

```
fruits = ['apple', 'banana', 'cherry']
for fruit in fruits:
    print(fruit)
```

Output:

```
apple
banana
cherry
```

Example#2: Looping through a string

```
name = 'John'
for character in name:
    print(character)
```

Output:

```
J
o
h
n
```

Example#3: Looping through a dictionary

```
person = {'name': 'John', 'age': 25}
for key, value in person.items():
```

```
    print(key, value)
```

Output:

```
name John
age 25
```

While Loops

While loops are used to execute a set of instructions repeatedly as long as a certain condition is true. The syntax of the while loop is as follows:

```
while condition:
    # Code to be executed
```

The while loop first checks the condition. If the condition is true, it executes the code block. Then, it checks the condition again and continues until the condition becomes false.

Example#1: Looping until a condition is met

```
count = 0
while count < 5:
    print(count)
    count += 1
```

Output:

```
0
1
2
3
4
```

Example#2: Looping until a user enters a valid input

```
valid_input = False
while not valid_input:
    user_input = input('Enter a number: ')
    if user_input.isdigit():
```

```
        print('You entered:', user_input)
        valid_input = True
    else:
        print('Invalid input, please try again')
```

Output:

```
Enter a number: abc
Invalid input, please try again
Enter a number: 123
You entered: 123
```

Example#3: Looping until a user decides to quit

```
while True:
    user_input = input('Enter a number or type "quit" to exit: ')
    if user_input == 'quit':
        break
    elif user_input.isdigit():
        print('You entered:', user_input)
    else:
        print('Invalid input, please try again')
```

Output:

```
Enter a number or type "quit" to exit: abc
Invalid input, please try again
Enter a number or type "quit" to exit: 123
You entered: 123
Enter a number or type "quit" to exit: quit
```

Overall, loops in Python are essential for executing a set of instructions repeatedly. The for loop is used to iterate over a sequence or iterable object, while the while loop is used to execute a set of instructions repeatedly as long as a certain condition is true. Understanding loops and their syntax is essential for writing efficient and effective Python programs.

Working with Functions

Functions in Python are reusable blocks of code that perform a specific task. They are used to reduce code duplication and to make code easier to read and maintain. In this tutorial, we will discuss the basics of functions in Python with practical examples.

Defining Functions

The syntax for defining a function in Python is as follows:

```
def function_name(parameters):
    # Code to be executed
    return return_value
```

The function definition starts with the def keyword, followed by the name of the function, and a set of parentheses that may or may not contain parameters. The code to be executed by the function is indented and followed by an optional return statement that specifies the value to be returned by the function.

Example#1: A simple function that adds two numbers

```
def add_numbers(a, b):
    result = a + b
    return result
```

Example#2: A function that prints a greeting message

```
def say_hello(name):
    print(f'Hello, {name}!')
```

Calling Functions

To call a function in Python, you simply write the name of the function followed by a set of parentheses that may or may not contain arguments.

Example#1: Calling the add_numbers function

```
result = add_numbers(2, 3)
print(result)
```

Output:

```
5
```

Example#2: Calling the say_hello function

```
say_hello('John')
```

Output:

```
Hello, John!
```

Default Arguments

In Python, you can define default values for function parameters. If a value is not passed for a parameter, the default value is used instead.

Example#1: A function with default arguments

```
def say_hello(name='World'):
    print(f'Hello, {name}!')
```

Example#2: Calling the say_hello function with default arguments

```
say_hello()
say_hello('John')
```

Output:

```
Hello, World!
Hello, John!
```

Variable-length Arguments

In Python, you can define functions that accept a variable number of arguments. There are two ways to define variable-length arguments: using the *args syntax to pass a variable number of positional arguments, or using the **kwargs syntax to pass a variable number of keyword arguments.

Example#1: A function with variable-length positional arguments

```
def print_args(*args):
```

```
    for arg in args:
        print(arg)
```

Example#2: Calling the print_args function with variable-length positional arguments

```
print_args(1, 2, 3)
```

Output:

```
1
2
3
```

Example#3: A function with variable-length keyword arguments

```
def print_kwargs(**kwargs):
    for key, value in kwargs.items():
        print(key, value)
```

Example#4: Calling the print_kwargs function with variable-length keyword arguments

```
print_kwargs(name='John', age=25)
```

Output:

```
name John
age 25
```

Lambda Functions

Lambda functions, also known as anonymous functions, are small, one-line functions that can be defined without a name. They are useful for writing quick and simple functions that are only used once.

Example#1: A lambda function that doubles a number

```
double = lambda x: x * 2
result = double(3)
```

```
print(result)
```

Output:

```
6
```

Example#2: A lambda function that sorts a list of tuples by the second element

```
students = [('John', 25), ('Mary', 23), ('Tom', 27)]
students.sort(key=lambda x: x[1])
print(students)
```

Output:

```
[('Mary', 23), ('John', 25), ('Tom', 27)]
```

Recursion

In Python, you can define functions that call themselves. These functions are called recursive functions, and they are useful for solving problems that can be broken down into smaller subproblems.

Example#1: A recursive function that calculates the factorial of a number

```
def factorial(n):
  if n == 0:
    return 1
  else:
    return n * factorial(n - 1)
```

Example#2: Calling the factorial function

```
result = factorial(5)
print(result)
```

Output:

```
120
```

Global and Local Variables

In Python, variables defined inside a function are local to that function and cannot be accessed outside of it. Variables defined outside of a function are global and can be accessed anywhere in the program.

Example#1: A function that modifies a global variable

```
count = 0

def increment_count():
    global count
    count += 1

increment_count()
increment_count()
increment_count()
print(count)
```

Output:

```
3
```

Example#2: A function that uses a local variable

```
def square(x):
    result = x ** 2
    return result

print(square(5))
```

Output:

```
25
```

Function Arguments

In Python, function arguments can be passed by reference or by value. When an argument is passed by reference, any changes made to the argument inside the function are reflected outside the function. When an argument is passed by value, any changes made to the argument inside the function are not reflected outside the function.

Example#1: A function that modifies a list passed by reference

```
def add_to_list(numbers, x):
  numbers.append(x)

my_list = [1, 2, 3]
add_to_list(my_list, 4)
print(my_list)
```

Output:

```
[1, 2, 3, 4]
```

Example#2: A function that does not modify an integer passed by value

```
def square(x):
  x = x ** 2
  return x

number = 5
square(number)
print(number)
```

Output:

```
5
```

Nested Functions

In Python, you can define functions inside other functions. These functions are called nested functions, and they are useful for organizing code and limiting the scope of variables.

Example#1: A function that defines a nested function

```
def outer_function():
  def inner_function():
    print('This is the inner function')
  inner_function()

outer_function()
```

Output:

```
This is the inner function
```

Example#2: A function that returns a nested function

```
def outer_function():
  def inner_function():
    print('This is the inner function')
  return inner_function

function = outer_function()
function()
```

Output:

```
This is the inner function
```

Overall, functions are an essential part of Python programming. They allow us to write reusable code, organize our programs, and solve problems more efficiently. Understanding the basics of functions is crucial for any Python developer, and the examples provided in this tutorial should help you get started.

Summary

In this chapter, we covered a wide range of topics related to Python programming. We started by discussing the basics of Python, including its history, features, and use cases. Python is a popular high-level programming language that is used for a wide range of tasks, including web development, data analysis, machine learning, and more. It is known for its simplicity, readability, and flexibility.

We then covered the fundamental concepts of Python, such as variables, data types, operators, and control structures. Variables are used to store data, while data types define the kind of data that can be stored. Operators are used to perform operations on data, while control structures, such as if-else statements and loops, are used to control the flow of a program.

CHAPTER 2: FILE HANDLING AND MODULES IN PYTHON

File Handling

File handling is an important aspect of programming, and it refers to the various operations that can be performed on files such as reading from, writing to, and modifying files. In Python, you can perform file handling operations using the built-in file handling functions.

There are three main file handling modes in Python: read, write, and append. In the read mode, you can read data from a file. In the write mode, you can create a new file or overwrite an existing file with new data. In the append mode, you can add new data to an existing file.

Opening and Closing Files

To perform file handling operations, you need to open a file first. You can do this using the open() function, which takes two arguments: the name of the file and the mode in which you want to open the file.

Example#1: Opening a file in read mode

```
file = open('example.txt', 'r')
```

Example#2: Opening a file in write mode

```
file = open('example.txt', 'w')
```

Once you have finished performing operations on the file, you should close the file using the close() function.

Example#3: Closing a file

```
file.close()
```

Reading from Files

In Python, you can read data from files using the read() function. This function reads the entire file and returns the contents of the file as a string.

Example#1: Reading from a file

```
file = open('example.txt', 'r')
contents = file.read()
print(contents)
file.close()
```

Output:

```
This is an example file.
It contains some text.
```

You can also read data from a file line by line using the readline() function.

Example#2: Reading from a file line by line

```
file = open('example.txt', 'r')
line = file.readline()
while line != '':
  print(line)
  line = file.readline()
file.close()
```

Output:

```
This is an example file.

It contains some text.
```

Writing to Files

In Python, you can write data to files using the write() function. This function writes data to a file and returns the number of characters written to the file.

Example#1: Writing to a file

```
file = open('example.txt', 'w')
file.write('This is a new line.\n')
file.write('This is another new line.\n')
file.close()
```

Example#2: Writing to a file using a list of strings

```
lines = ['This is a new line.\n', 'This is another new line.\n']
file = open('example.txt', 'w')
file.writelines(lines)
file.close()
```

Both examples produce the same output:

```
This is a new line.
This is another new line.
```

Appending to Files

In Python, you can append data to a file using the append() function. This function adds data to the end of a file without overwriting any existing data.

Example: Appending to a file

```
file = open('example.txt', 'a')
file.write('This is a third line.\n')
file.close()
```

Output:

```
This is a new line.
This is another new line.
This is a third line.
```

With Statement

In Python, you can use the with statement to open a file and automatically close it when you are finished performing operations on the file. This is a safer and more efficient way of working with files, as it ensures that the file is properly closed even if an error occurs.

Example#1: Using the with statement to read from a file

```
with open('example.txt', 'r') as file:
  contents = file.read()
  print(contents)
```

Output:

```
This is a new line.
```

```
This is another new line.
This is a third line.
```

Example#2: Using the with statement to write to a file

```
with open('example.txt', 'w') as file:
    file.write('This is a new line.\n')
    file.write('This is another new line.\n')
```

Example#3: Using the with statement to append to a file

```
with open('example.txt', 'a') as file:
    file.write('This is a third line.\n')
```

Exception Handling:

When working with files, it is important to handle exceptions properly in case an error occurs. This can be done using a try and except block.

Example: Handling exceptions when reading from a file

```
try:
    file = open('example.txt', 'r')
    contents = file.read()
    print(contents)
except FileNotFoundError:
    print('File not found')
finally:
    file.close()
```

Output:

```
This is a new line.
This is another new line.
This is a third line.
```

In the above example, we use a try block to attempt to read from a file. If the file is not found, we handle the FileNotFoundError exception using an except block. We also use a finally block to ensure that the file is properly closed, even if an error occurs.

To sum it up, file handling is an important aspect of programming, and Python provides a range of built-in functions that allow you to perform various file handling operations. By using the open() function to open a file, and the read(), write(), and append() functions to perform operations on the file, you can easily read from and write to files in Python. Additionally, the with statement can be used to automatically close a file once you have finished working with it, and exception handling can be used to handle errors that may occur when working with files.

Utilizing Modules

A module is a file that uses the Python programming language and contains statements and definitions. One way to think of it is as a mechanism for organising and reusing code. Python programmes can take advantage of the functions, classes, and variables stored in modules because modules can be imported into other Python programmes.

Modules, in their conceptual form, offer a way to partition large computer programmes into a number of smaller, more manageable parts. Developers can more easily maintain and debug their code when it is organised into modules, and they can reuse code across multiple projects if they organise their code this way.

Because modules can be imported into other programmes, they allow programmers to avoid writing code twice as often, which is another way that modules promote code reusability.

Python offers a vast library of modules that can be used for a variety of purposes, including working with files, establishing and maintaining a network, and processing data. The code that a developer writes can be encapsulated in their own modules, which they can then share with other developers.

Creating a Module

To create a module, simply write your Python code in a file with a .py extension. For example, let's create a module named my_module.py with the following code:

```
# my_module.py

def hello(name):
    print(f"Hello, {name}!")
```

This module contains a function named hello that takes a name as an argument and prints a greeting.

Importing a Module

Once you have created a module, you can import it into other Python scripts or modules. There are several ways to import a module:

import statement

Use the import statement followed by the name of the module to import the entire module.
Example:

```
import my_module

my_module.hello("John")
```

Output:

```
Hello, John!
```

from statement

Use the from statement followed by the name of the module and the keyword import to import specific functions or variables from a module.
Example:

```
from my_module import hello

hello("Jane")
```

Output:

```
Hello, Jane!
```

Built-In Modules

Python also comes with a set of built-in modules that provide useful functionality out of the box. These modules can be imported just like any other module.
Example: Using the random module to generate a random number

```
import random
```

```
number = random.randint(1, 10)
print(number)
```

Output:

```
7
```

In the above example, we import the random module and use the randint() function to generate a random integer between 1 and 10.

Creating Packages

Python modules can be organized into packages, which are simply directories containing a __init__.py file and one or more Python modules. Packages can be nested within other packages to create a hierarchical organization of code.
Example:

```
my_package/
├── __init__.py
├── module1.py
└── module2.py
```

In the above code, my_package is a package that contains two Python modules, module1.py and module2.py. The __init__.py file is required to indicate that the directory is a package.

Standard Library Modules

Python also comes with a large standard library of modules that provide additional functionality for tasks such as working with dates and times, performing network operations, and parsing XML and JSON data. These modules can be imported just like any other module.
Example: Using the datetime module to work with dates and times

```
import datetime

today = datetime.date.today()
print(today)
```

Output:

```
2023-02-22
```

In the above example, we import the datetime module and use the date.today() function to get the current date.

To summarize it in short, Python modules provide a way to organize code into reusable units that can be imported into other modules or scripts. By using the import and from statements, you can easily import modules and their functions and variables into your Python code. Python also comes with a set of built-in modules and a large standard library of modules that provide additional functionality for a wide range of tasks. By organizing your code into packages, you can create a hierarchical organization of code that makes it easy to manage and maintain.

My First Python Script

Let us create a simple Python script that demonstrates some of the concepts we've covered in this chapter.
The script will perform the following tasks:

- Prompt the user for their name and age
- Calculate the user's year of birth
- Check if the user is old enough to vote
- Write the user's name, age, year of birth, and voting eligibility to a file

Following is the script:

```
import datetime

def calculate_year_of_birth(age):
  current_year = datetime.date.today().year
  return current_year - age

def check_voting_eligibility(age):
  return age >= 18

def main():
  name = input("What is your name? ")
  age = int(input("What is your age? "))
  year_of_birth = calculate_year_of_birth(age)
  eligible_to_vote = check_voting_eligibility(age)

  with open("user_info.txt", "w") as file:
```

```
        file.write(f"Name: {name}\n")
        file.write(f"Age: {age}\n")
        file.write(f"Year of birth: {year_of_birth}\n")
        if eligible_to_vote:
            file.write("Eligible to vote: Yes\n")
        else:
            file.write("Eligible to vote: No\n")

if __name__ == "__main__":
    main()
```

Let us see how the script works as below:

- We import the datetime module, which we use in the calculate_year_of_birth function to get the current year.
- We define a calculate_year_of_birth function that takes an age as an argument and returns the year of birth.
- We define a check_voting_eligibility function that takes an age as an argument and returns True if the person is eligible to vote (i.e., 18 years or older).
- We define a main function that prompts the user for their name and age, calculates the year of birth and voting eligibility using the other functions, and writes the user's information to a file.
- We use the with statement to open the file user_info.txt in write mode, and we use the write method to write the user's information to the file.
- Finally, we use the if __name__ == "__main__" statement to call the main function when the script is run.
- When you run the script, it will prompt you for your name and age, and then create a file named user_info.txt with your information.

The contents of the file will look something like this:

```
Name: John
Age: 30
Year of birth: 1992
Eligible to vote: Yes
```

This your own first script demonstrates some of the key concepts you have learned, such as input/output, functions, modules, and file handling. You can use these concepts to create much more complex and powerful Python programs.

Summary

In this chapter, we discussed some of the most advanced features of Python, such as modules, and file handling. Modules are used to organize code into separate files and namespaces. File handling is used to read from and write to files, which can be useful for storing and retrieving data.

Throughout the chapter, we emphasized the importance of good programming practices, such as writing clean and readable code, commenting and documenting code, and using version control systems like Git. These practices can help make your code more maintainable, reliable, and scalable over time. Finally, we created a simple Python script that demonstrated some of the key concepts we discussed, such as input/output, functions, modules, and file handling. The script prompted the user for their name and age, calculated their year of birth and voting eligibility, and wrote their information to a file.

In summary, Python is known for its simplicity, flexibility, and readability, and it has a large and active community of developers and users. By mastering the fundamental concepts of Python, as well as some of the more advanced features and practical applications, you can become a skilled Python programmer and create a variety of useful and innovative applications.

Chapter 3: Preparing Network Automation Lab

Components of Network Automation Process

The process of automating network operations in order to reduce the amount of manual labour required for network management is referred to as network automation. In order to test and develop network automation scripts and tools, it is absolutely necessary to have network automation labs. In this chapter, we will talk about the various components of a network automation lab, as well as how these components work together to provide a streamlined experience for network automation. In addition, we will discuss how these components work together to provide a streamlined experience for network automation.

Network devices, a network emulator, an environment based on the Python programming language, and automation scripts are the standard elements that make up a network automation lab. When put together, these components produce a simulated network environment that can be put to use in the creation and testing of scripts for network automation. This environment can be used for a variety of purposes.

Network Devices

The hardware components known as "network devices" are what make it possible for devices connected to a computer network to communicate with one another. They make it easier for devices on a network to communicate with one another and gain access to shared resources by facilitating the transmission of data between the various components of a network.
There are many different kinds of network devices, each of which has its own particular function and part to play in the infrastructure of the network. Routers, switches, hubs, firewalls, and modems are just some of the devices that are used to create and maintain networks.

Due to the fact that they are in charge of directing traffic between various networks, routers are widely considered to be the most essential networking devices. They make use of routing tables to determine the most efficient route for data packets to take, taking into account information such as IP addresses and the topology of the network. Routers typically come equipped with a variety of interfaces, which enables them to connect to a wide variety of networks as well as devices. On the other hand, switches are what are used to connect different devices that are part of the same network. They use the MAC addresses to figure out where to send the data packets, which enables the devices to communicate directly with one another. Managed switches provide a higher level of control and more configuration options than unmanaged switches do. Switches can either be managed or unmanaged.

Hubs are a different kind of networking device that are used to connect devices that are already part of the same network. Hubs, on the other hand, do not care about the final destination of the data packets they receive; rather, they simply transmit them to all of the devices to which they are connected. Because of this, there is a potential for increased network traffic and congestion, which may result in hubs being utilised less frequently in the future. Firewalls are devices that can be installed on a network to prevent unauthorised access and malicious traffic from entering the system. They can be based on either hardware or software, and in order to block unwanted traffic while allowing legitimate traffic to pass through, they typically use a combination of rules, policies, and filters. These can be implemented in either form.

In order to connect a computer or other device to the internet, you will need to use a modem, which is a type of network device. They take the digital signals produced by a computer and convert them into analogue signals that can be sent over telephone lines or cable connections, thereby enabling users to connect to the internet through the medium of their internet service provider (ISP). Other types of network devices include access points, which are used to connect wireless devices to a network, and network interface cards, also known as NICs, which are used to connect devices to a network using a wired connection. Both of these types of devices are considered to be subtypes of network devices.

In general, network devices are essential components of modern computer networks because they enable devices to communicate with one another and access resources that are shared by the network. Network administrators are able to design and maintain network infrastructures that are efficient, secure, and reliable in order to meet the needs of their organisations if they have a thorough understanding of the various types of network devices and the functions they perform.

Network Emulator

A network emulator is a piece of software that gives developers and IT professionals the ability to simulate and test real-world network conditions within a simulated network environment. In order to test the performance of applications and network infrastructure under real-world conditions, it simulates various types of network connections, bandwidths, latencies, and packet loss rates. The performance of applications under varying network types and conditions can be tested using a network emulator, the impact of network changes can be verified, and service level agreements for network-dependent applications can be ensured using a network emulator. These are just some of the many possible applications of a network emulator (SLAs).

A network emulator is typically made up of both software and hardware components that, when combined, serve the purpose of simulating the workings of a network. The software component is in charge of providing the tools necessary to configure and control the network conditions, while the hardware component is in charge of creating the actual physical environment in which the network emulation will take place.

Users are granted the ability to configure various network parameters through the use of the software component of a network emulator. These parameters include bandwidth, latency, packet loss rate, and network topology. In addition to this, it offers tools that can generate traffic and measure performance metrics like throughput, latency, and jitter. When using a network emulator, developers and IT professionals are able to test their applications and infrastructure in an environment that is both safe and under their control. This is one of the most significant advantages of using a network emulator. This can help to identify potential problems before they occur in production environments, which can help to save time as well as reduce costs associated with downtime and lost revenue.

The ability of users to replicate different network conditions, such as those that are present in environments that are remotely located or congested, is another advantage that comes with the utilisation of a network emulator. This can be helpful in identifying and fixing performance issues, some of which might not be obvious when the network conditions are ideal. Emulators of a network can also be used to test and optimise network infrastructure, such as routers, switches, and firewalls. This is another use for network simulators. Users are able to identify potential bottlenecks and optimise the configuration of network devices by simulating different network conditions and identifying potential bottlenecks.

In a nutshell, a network emulator is a tool that gives programmers and IT professionals the ability to simulate various network conditions and test applications and infrastructure in an environment that is both safe and under their direct control. It is possible to use it to identify and resolve performance issues, optimise network infrastructure, and ensure that network-dependent applications meet service level agreements using this tool.

Python Environment

Python is a well-liked programming language for network automation because of its user-friendliness, adaptability, and extensive repository of libraries developed by third parties. A Python environment includes not only the Python programming language but also any additional libraries or tools that are necessary to create and execute Python scripts. The Python environment in a lab dedicated to network automation will typically consist of the

Python interpreter, a package manager such as pip, and any third-party libraries that are necessary for performing tasks related to network automation.

Automation Scripts

Automation scripts are Python scripts that automate network tasks such as configuration management, network monitoring, and troubleshooting. These scripts use APIs and protocols such as NETCONF, RESTCONF, SNMP, and SSH to interact with network devices and retrieve or modify network configuration data. Automation scripts can be run on-demand or scheduled to run at specific intervals, providing continuous network monitoring and maintenance.

Putting It All Together

Choosing a network emulator should be the first thing you do when you're getting ready to set up a network automation lab. Popular emulators include GNS3, EVE-NG, and VIRL. The emulator needs to be set up so that it can generate virtual network devices that can simulate the operating environment of the network. It is recommended that the simulated network topology be used to connect the virtual devices so that it accurately reflects the real-world network environment.

After that, a Python environment needs to be created on the laboratory computer. Either by using a Python distribution like Anaconda or by manually installing Python and any necessary libraries, this can be accomplished. Anaconda is one example of a Python distribution. A package manager, such as pip, should be included in the Python environment in order to facilitate the installation of any necessary third-party libraries. Scripts for automation can be developed and tested in the lab environment once the Python environment has been set up. Text editors or integrated development environments (IDEs) like PyCharm or Visual Studio Code can be used to write automation scripts. Another option is to use a simple text editor. In order to interact with network devices, the scripts ought to make use of Python libraries such as Netmiko, Nornir, or PyEZ.

Automation scripts can be executed by hand, or they can be programmed to execute at predetermined intervals using tools like cron or the Windows Task Scheduler. Scripts may be executed either on the system used in the laboratory or on a server specifically designated for automation.

Benefits of Network Automation Lab

Network engineers and administrators stand to gain from the establishment of a network automation lab in more ways than one.
To begin, it enables the development and testing of automation scripts in an environment that is under controlled conditions. This decreases the likelihood of errors or disruptions occurring on the production network.
Second, it offers a sandbox environment in which new network technologies and configurations can be tested before being introduced into the live network.

Last but not least, it makes it possible to automate routine network tasks, which in turn reduces the amount of manual labour needed for network management and maintenance.

Therefore, a network automation lab is a necessary piece of equipment for network engineers and administrators who have the goal of automating network tasks in order to reduce the amount of manual labour needed for network management. Virtual or emulated network devices, a network emulator, an environment running Python, and automation scripts are the standard components of the lab. Engineers and administrators can develop and test automation scripts in a controlled environment by establishing a network automation lab. This lowers the risk of errors or disruptions occurring on the production network and allows for the testing of new network technologies and configurations. Automating routine network tasks is also made possible by this setup.

To get started with the process of establishing a network automation lab, select a network emulator that is able to simulate the network environment, establish a Python environment that contains all of the necessary libraries, and create automation scripts by making use of Python libraries like Netmiko, Nornir, or PyEZ. Overall, make use of applications like cron or the Windows Task Scheduler to automate mundane network tasks and set up scripts to run at predetermined intervals.

An ideal environment for network engineers and administrators to develop and test automation scripts, reduce the amount of manual labour required for network management, and streamline routine network tasks is provided by a network automation lab.

Install NS3 Network Simulator

NS-3 is an open-source discrete-event network simulator that can be used to simulate and analyze various network protocols and scenarios. In this chapter, we will go through the practical steps to install NS-3 network simulator on Linux.

System Requirements

Before we start the installation, we need to ensure that the system meets the minimum requirements to run NS-3. The recommended system requirements are as follows:

Operating System: Linux (Ubuntu, Debian, Fedora, CentOS, other Linux distribution)
RAM: 2 GB
Processor: Dual-core or higher
Disk space: At least 5 GB free space

Install Required Dependencies

NS-3 has a number of dependencies that need to be installed before we can install NS-3. The following command will install the required dependencies:

For Ubuntu/Debian

```
sudo apt-get update
sudo apt-get install gcc g++ python python-dev mercurial bzr gdb valgrind gsl-bin libgsl-dev libgsl23 libgslcblas0 python-pygraphviz python-kiwi python-pygoocanvas python-gnome2 python-rsvg ipython
```

For Fedora:

```
sudo dnf install gcc-c++ python python-devel mercurial bzr gdb valgrind gsl gsl-devel gsl-static pygtk2-devel pygobject2-devel graphviz graphviz-gd python-pygraphviz pygtk2 libxml2 libxml2-devel libxml2-python PyQt4 PyQt4-devel qt4-devel qt4 qt-devel python-qwt5-qt4 python-qwt5-qt4-devel python-qwt5-qt4-doc PyQt4-doc PyQt4-qscintilla PyQt4-qscintilla-devel PyQt4-qscintilla-python PyQt4-devel PyQt4-webkit PyQt4-webkit-devel qt-webkit-devel qtwebkit-devel gnome-python2-gnomevfs gnome-python2-gnomevfs-devel gnome-python2-gnomekeyring gnome-python2-gnomekeyring-devel gnome-python2-extras gnome-python2-extras-devel gnome-python2-bonobo gnome-python2-bonobo-devel gnome-python2-canvas gnome-python2-canvas-devel gnome-python2-gtkhtml2 gnome-python2-gtkhtml2-devel python-numeric python-numpy python-scipy python-matplotlib
```

```
python-matplotlib-doc python-matplotlib-tk python-matplotlib-wx python-
setuptools python-twisted python-zope-interface PyQt4-qsci-devel PyQt4-qsci
```

Download NS-3

NS-3 can be downloaded from the official website or cloned from the Git repository. We will use the Git repository to download NS-3.

Open a terminal and navigate to the directory where you want to download NS-3. Then, run the following command to clone the Git repository:

```
git clone https://gitlab.com/nsnam/ns-3-allinone.git
```

Step 4: Build NS-3

After downloading NS-3, we need to build it. Change the directory to the NS-3-allinone directory and run the following command:

```
cd ns-3-allinone
./build.py --enable-examples --enable-tests
```

The above command will build NS-3 with examples and tests. If you want to build NS-3 without examples and tests, use the following command:

```
./build.py
```

Note: The build process may take some time depending on your system specifications.

Step 5: Test NS-3

After building NS-3, we can test it by running a sample program. Change the directory to the NS-3 directory and run the following command:

```
cd ns-3-dev
./
waf --run hello-simulator
```

This command will run the "hello-simulator" program, which is a simple program that creates a simulation and runs it.

If everything is working properly, you should see the following output:

```
Running "build" task
Running build
No tests defined.
Running "run" task
Running run
Hello Simulator
Simulation completed successfully
```

Congratulations! You have successfully installed NS-3 on Linux.

Step 6: Using NS-3

To use NS-3, you can start by exploring the example programs that come with the simulator. The examples are located in the "examples/" directory.

For example, you can run the following command to simulate a simple point-to-point network:

```
cd examples/tutorial/first
./waf --run scratch/first
```

This will create a simulation of a point-to-point network with two nodes, and the output will show the packets being transmitted between the nodes.

To create your own simulations, you can use the NS-3 API, which provides a rich set of classes and functions for creating and configuring network topologies, traffic generators, and protocol stacks.

To conclude, NS-3 is a powerful network simulator that can be used to simulate and analyze various network scenarios. In this chapter, we went through the practical steps to install NS-3 on Linux. We also explored how to test NS-3 and use it to create simple simulations.

Install Python

Python is a popular programming language that is widely used for network automation. In this chapter, we will go through the practical steps to install Python for network automation on a Linux system.

Update System

Before installing Python, we need to update the system to ensure that we have the latest software packages. Open a terminal and run the following command to update the system:

```
sudo apt-get update
```

Install Python

Python is pre-installed on most Linux distributions. However, we can install the latest version of Python by running the following command:

```
sudo apt-get install python3
```

This command will install Python 3, which is the latest version of Python.

Install pip

Pip is a package manager for Python that is used to install and manage Python packages. To install pip, run the following command:

```
sudo apt-get install python3-pip
```

Install paramiko, Netmiko and Nornir

Python has a number of libraries that are specifically designed for network automation. Some of the popular libraries include:

- paramiko: A library for SSH connectivity
- Netmiko: A library for network device access over SSH
- Nornir: A library for network automation and orchestration

To install these libraries, run the following command:

```
sudo pip3 install paramiko netmiko nornir
```

This command will install the paramiko, netmiko, and nornir libraries.

Install Virtual Environment

Virtual environment is a tool that is used to create isolated Python environments. This is useful when working on multiple projects with different dependencies. To install virtual environment, run the following command:

```
sudo pip3 install virtualenv
```

Create Virtual Environment

To create a virtual environment, run the following command:

```
virtualenv myenv
```

This command will create a virtual environment named "myenv" in the current directory.

Activate the Virtual Environment

To activate the virtual environment, run the following command:

```
source myenv/bin/activate
```

This command will activate the virtual environment, and you will see the name of the virtual environment in the command prompt.

Install Python Libraries in Virtual Environment

To install Python libraries in the virtual environment, run the following command:

```
pip3 install paramiko netmiko nornir
```

This command will install the paramiko, netmiko, and nornir libraries in the virtual environment.

Deactivate the Virtual Environment

To deactivate the virtual environment, run the following command:

```
deactivate
```

This command will deactivate the virtual environment.

By following these steps, you can start developing network automation scripts using Python.

Install Visual Studio Code

Visual Studio Code (VS Code) is a popular code editor that supports many programming languages, including Python. It is a lightweight and versatile editor that has a rich set of features, such as code highlighting, debugging, and code completion. In this chapter, we will go through the practical steps to install and configure VS Code for network automation lab.

Download and Install VS Code

To download and install VS Code,

- go to the official VS Code website at https://code.visualstudio.com/download.
- Select the appropriate installer for your operating system and click the download button.
- Once the download is complete, run the installer and follow the installation wizard.

Install Python Extension

To use VS Code for Python development, we need to install the Python extension. To install the extension, follow these steps:

- Open VS Code.
- Click on the Extensions icon on the left-hand side of the screen (or press Ctrl + Shift + X).
- Type "Python" in the search box.
- Click the install button for the "Python" extension.
- Wait for the installation to complete.

Configure Python Interpreter

Once the Python extension is installed, we need to configure the Python interpreter that VS Code will use for our Python projects.

To configure the Python interpreter, follow these steps:

- Open VS Code.
- Click on the Settings icon on the left-hand side of the screen (or press Ctrl + ,).

- Type "Python Path" in the search box.
- Click the "Edit in settings.json" button.
- Add the following line to the settings.json file:

```
"python.pythonPath": "/usr/bin/python3"
```

Note that the path may be different on your system, depending on where Python is installed.

Create Python Project

To create a Python project in VS Code, follow these steps:

- Open VS Code.
- Click on the File menu and select "New Folder".
- Choose a name for the folder and create it.
- Click on the File menu and select "Open Folder".
- Select the folder that you just created.
- Click on the File menu and select "New File".
- Choose a name for the file and save it with a ".py" extension.

Write Python Code

To write Python code in VS Code, follow these steps:

- Open the Python file that you created in the previous step.
- Start writing your Python code.
- Use the VS Code features, such as code highlighting, debugging, and code completion, to help you write your code.

Run Python Code

To run Python code in VS Code, follow these steps:

- Open the Python file that you created.
- Click on the Run menu and select "Run Without Debugging" (or press Ctrl + F5).
- VS Code will run the Python code and display the output in the terminal.

In this section, we went through the practical steps to install and configure VS Code for network automation lab. By following the above steps, you can start developing Python scripts for network automation in a professional and efficient way.

Summary

In this chapter, we discussed the process of setting up a network automation lab using Python. We first discussed the importance of automation in network management and the benefits it offers, such as increased efficiency and reduced errors.

We then talked about the components required for setting up a network automation lab, such as NS3 emulator, Python, Virtual Environment and VS Code. We went on to discuss the process of installing the NS3 emulator on a Linux system and configuring it for use. This involved downloading and installing the emulator, as well as setting up the necessary dependencies and environment variables. Next, we talked about installing Python and configuring it for use with network automation libraries. This involved setting up a virtual environment, installing the required packages, and testing the installation.

Chapter 4: Configuring Libraries and Lab Components

Nornir

The Nornir framework is a Python-based automation tool that was developed specifically for network automation tasks. It is a free and open-source library that offers a straightforward and adaptable method of automating network tasks. This makes it possible for network engineers to concentrate on the tasks at hand without being distracted by concerns regarding the underlying infrastructure.

Architecture of Nornir

Architecture of Nornir: The architecture of Nornir is based on the idea of using plugins in various places. A framework's functionality can be extended with the help of a small piece of code called a plugin. Plugins can either add new functionality or replace functionality that already exists.

In Nornir, the following are the three primary categories of plugins:

Inventory Plugin

This includes the hostname of the device, its IP address, and any other information that may be pertinent. YAML, CSV, and SQL are all formats that can be used as inventory plugins.

Processor Plugin

A processor plugin's job is to ensure that the tasks assigned to it are carried out successfully on the devices. The results are provided after a task and a list of devices have been provided to it. SSH, NETCONF, and REST are a few examples of processor plugins that are available.

Result Plugin

It then saves the results in a location from which other plugins can quickly retrieve them in order to process them further. SQLite, JSON, and CSV are a few examples of different types of result plugins.

The following are the primary elements that make up Nornir's architecture:

- A piece of code that carries out a particular operation on a device is referred to as a task. Any programming language may be used to create tasks, and a processor plugin is responsible for carrying out their instructions.
- An inventory is a list of all of the different devices that are currently being managed. You have the option of manually creating the inventory, or you can use an inventory plugin to do it automatically.

- A processor is the component of a device that is in charge of putting instructions into action. Nornir comes with a number of different processor plugins already installed, but users are also able to create their own bespoke processor plugins.
- The output of a task that has been carried out on a device is referred to as the result of the task. The results are saved in a result plugin, and other plugins have the ability to access those results.

Significance of Nornir

Nornir is an essential library for network automation for a number of reasons, including the following:

Simplifies Network Automation

Nornir is able to simplify network automation because it offers a framework that is both straightforward and versatile for the automation of network tasks. Because of this, network engineers are able to concentrate on their primary responsibilities without being distracted by the infrastructure beneath them.

Multiple Platforms Are Supported

Nornir is compatible with a wide variety of network platforms, including those developed by Cisco, Juniper, and Arista. Because of this, it is an excellent option for businesses that operate in a network environment that is highly diverse.

Open-Source

Nornir is a library that is an open-source project, which means that it is freely accessible online and can be modified to fulfil a variety of requirements. Because of this, it is an excellent option for businesses that want to automate the tasks associated with their network but do not want to incur significant costs.

Extensible

Because Nornir's architecture is built around the idea of plugins, it is very simple to add new functionality to the framework. This feature is known as "extensibility." Because of this, businesses now have the ability to develop bespoke plugins that can be used to automate particular network tasks.

Integration with Other Libraries

The fact that Nornir is compatible with other Python libraries, such as Netmiko and Napalm, makes it much simpler to automate various network-related tasks. For instance, Netmiko can be used to automate network devices that are based on SSH, whereas Napalm can be used to automate network devices that are based on NETCONF.

Centralized Point of Access

Nornir offers a centralised point of access for managing and automating network tasks. This eliminates the need for network engineers to become proficient in a wide variety of programming languages and frameworks in order to automate network processes.

In a simple terms, Nornir is an open-source Python library that was designed to make network automation more user-friendly by delivering an adaptable and scalable infrastructure for automating various network-related tasks. The framework's functionality can be easily extended thanks to the fact that its architecture is centred on the idea of plugins. Nornir is compatible with a diverse selection of networks.

Paramiko

A Python library known as Paramiko offers an approach that is both straightforward and risk-free for automating SSH (Secure Shell) connections and file transfers. It is a library that is available for free and is utilised extensively in the field of network automation for a variety of tasks, including the backing up of configurations, the upgrading of software, and the execution of commands on remote devices.

Architecture of Paramiko

The Architecture of Paramiko The architecture of Paramiko is centred on the following two primary components:

SSH Client

An SSH connection with a remote device must be established and kept active by the SSH client. The SSH client is responsible for both of these tasks. The paramiko is utilised here. The SSH connection and the paramiko are both managed by the transport class. Class named SFTPClient that handles managing file transfers.

SSH Server

The SSH server is in charge of managing any incoming SSH connections, and its responsibilities include this. The paramiko is utilised here. Class named ServerInterface that is responsible for handling incoming requests and the paramiko. The Channel class is used to manage how commands are carried out.

In order to facilitate communication between SSH clients and servers, Paramiko offers a number of classes and methods. These are the following:

- Establishing and managing SSH connections can be done with the help of the paramiko.SSHClient class. It makes it possible to connect to an SSH server, run commands, and transfer files using the methods that it provides.
- The Transport class is responsible for managing the underlying SSH connection. It offers procedures for establishing a connection, authenticating both the client and the server, and encrypting data.
- The class, called paramiko.SFTPClient, is utilised during the process of transferring files over an SSH connection. It offers functionality for the uploading and downloading of files, the creation of directories, and the configuration of file permissions.
- There is another class responsible for handling incoming SSH requests and is referred to as paramiko.ServerInterface. It offers procedures for handling authentication, carrying out commands, and managing channels.
- And, the last and final class responsible for managing the execution of commands on remote devices, and its name is paramiko.Channel. It offers methods for transmitting and receiving data, as well as managing the standard input/output/error streams and controlling the execution of the command.

Significance of Paramiko

There are many reasons why this Paramiko library is so important for network automation:

Secure

Automate SSH connections and file transfers in a secure manner with Paramiko, which offers an encrypted method for doing so. It employs robust algorithms for encryption and provides means for safely managing authentication and encryption keys.

Lightweight

The Paramiko library is a lightweight option because it has a small footprint and does not rely on a large number of other packages for its functionality. Because of this, it can be easily installed and utilised in a diverse collection of network automation settings.

Cross-platform

Paramiko is a library that can be used on a variety of different operating systems, including Windows, Linux, and macOS. It is considered to be cross-platform. Because of this, it is an excellent option for businesses that operate in a network environment that is highly diverse.

East-to-use

Simple and straightforward application programming interface (API) offered by Paramiko for automating SSH connections and file transfers. Because of this, it is much simpler for network engineers to begin automating their networks without having to first become proficient in a variety of difficult programming languages or frameworks.

Configurable

The architecture of Paramiko was built with configurability and extensibility in mind from the start. This makes it possible for companies to personalise the library to meet the requirements of their particular operations, such as developing bespoke authentication procedures or integrating with additional network automation tools.

Integration with Other Libraries

Other Python libraries, such as Fabric and Ansible, can be used with Paramiko thanks to its integration with those libraries. Because these libraries provide additional functionality for managing SSH connections and executing commands on remote devices, the process of automating network tasks is facilitated as a result, making the process simpler.

To sum up, Paramiko is a small, safe, and platform-independent Python library that offers an easy-to-use application programming interface (API) for scripting SSH connections and file transfers. Because its architecture is intended to be both customizable and extensible, it is an excellent option for businesses that need to automate their complex networks and has been designed to do so. Because of its intuitive interface, extensive configurability, and seamless compatibility with a wide variety of libraries, Paramiko has emerged as a pivotal tool for various network automation endeavours.

Netmiko

Python's Netmiko library is a useful tool for streamlining network automation because it offers a unified interface to network devices that can be accessed via secure shell connections. It is constructed on top of Paramiko and is compatible with a wide variety of network devices, including those manufactured by Cisco, Juniper, Arista, and many others. For network automation, Netmiko provides a standardised application programming interface (API) that is simple to work with and abstracts away the complexity of interacting with various devices.

Architecture of Netmiko

The architecture of Netmiko is centred on three primary components, which are as follows:

Driver for Device

The driver for the device is in charge of managing the communication that takes place between Netmiko and the network device. It is a Python class that implements a set of methods for sending and receiving commands, parsing output, and handling errors. These methods can be found in the class's documentation.

Connection Handler

The connection handler is in charge of managing the SSH connection to the network device. This responsibility falls on the connection handler. It does this by establishing and maintaining the SSH connection with the help of the Paramiko library, which also provides methods for logging in and out of the SSH session as well as managing it.

Command Handler

The command handler is in charge of managing the execution of commands on the network device, and its responsibilities include this oversight. It does this by utilising the connection handler so that commands can be sent to the device and the output can be received. It also provides methods for handling errors and parsing the output.

Netmiko gives users access to a variety of device drivers for a wide variety of network devices, such as Cisco IOS, Cisco ASA, Juniper JunOS, Arista EOS, and a great deal more besides. Each device driver is responsible for implementing a set of methods that are unique to the device being driven. These methods may include sending and receiving commands, parsing output, and handling errors.

Significance of Netmiko

The Netmiko library is an important component of network automation for following features:

Unified Interface to Network Devices

Netmiko is able to simplify network automation by providing a unified interface to SSH connections for network devices. Automating tasks for network engineers, such as configuring devices, backing up configurations, and monitoring network performance, is made simpler as a result of this.

Supports Wide Variety of Devices

Netmiko is compatible with a wide variety of network devices, including those made by Cisco, Juniper, and Arista, amongst others. Because of this, it is an excellent option for businesses that operate in a network environment that is highly diverse.

Easy API Integration

Interacting with network devices is made easy with Netmiko's straightforward and well-documented application programming interface (API). Because of this, it is much simpler for network engineers to begin automating their networks without having to first become proficient in a variety of difficult programming languages or frameworks.

Configurable

The architecture of Netmiko was built with configurability and extensibility in mind from the start. This gives companies the ability to modify the library to meet the requirements of their particular projects, such as developing bespoke device drivers or integrating with a variety of other network automation tools.

Cross-platform

The Netmiko library is a cross-platform library, which means that it is compatible with a wide variety of operating systems. These operating systems include Windows, Linux, and macOS. Because of this, it is an excellent option for businesses that operate in a network environment that is highly diverse.

Supports Concurrent Connections

Netmiko supports concurrent connections to multiple devices. This makes it possible to automate tasks across a large number of devices simultaneously, which improves the efficiency of network automation tasks and reduces the amount of time required for those tasks.

To just summarize its importance, this is a Python library that offers a unified interface to network devices by means of secure shell connections. This helps to simplify the process of automating networks. Because its architecture is intended to be both customizable and extensible, it is an excellent option for businesses that need to automate their complex networks and has been designed to do so. Because of its user-friendliness, extensive configurability, and compatibility with a wide variety of devices, Netmiko is an essential tool for the completion of network automation tasks.

PyEZ

PyEZ is a Python library that makes network automation more straightforward for Juniper Networks's hardware. It offers a high-level application programming interface (API) for interacting with Junos OS, which is the name of the operating system that is used by Juniper Networks devices. PyEZ is a Python library that provides low-level access to the Junos OS command line interface (CLI), XML application programming interface (API), and NETCONF protocol. PyEZ is built on top of Junos PyEZ.

Architecture of PyEZ

The architecture of PyEZ is centred on four primary components, which are as follows:

Device

The object that is responsible for representing a Juniper Networks device in PyEZ is referred to as the device. It provides methods for connecting to the device, executing commands, retrieving and configuring the device's configuration, and additional functionality.

RPC

RPC stands for "Remote Procedure Call," and it is a protocol that enables applications to communicate with Junos OS by sending and receiving XML messages. RPC is also known as "Remote Procedure Call." PyEZ is an application programming interface (API) that simplifies the process of retrieving and configuring device information by providing a high-level interface for communicating with Junos OS via RPC.

Tables

Tables are used in PyEZ to represent structured data that is retrieved from Junos OS. Tables are used to organise the data. PyEZ offers a collection of predefined tables that can be used to retrieve a variety of different types of data, including interface statistics, routing tables, and more. Users are also able to define their very own bespoke tables, which can be used to retrieve particular information from the Junos OS.

Events

Events are used in PyEZ to monitor and react to changes in the state of a Juniper Networks device. Events are used to monitor and react to changes. PyEZ offers a collection of predefined events for monitoring a wide variety of events, including but not limited to changes in interface state, BGP route changes, and more. In addition, users have the ability to define their very own bespoke events for monitoring specific OS changes in Junos.

Significance of PyEZ

PyEZ is an essential library for network automation for a number of reasons, including the following:

Simplifies Network Automation

PyEZ is able to simplify network automation because it provides a high-level API for interacting with Junos OS. Network engineers will find it much simpler to automate tasks like configuring devices, retrieving information, and monitoring the performance of the network as a result of this.

Supports JunosOS

PyEZ was developed specifically for Juniper Networks devices that are operating under the Junos operating system, and it offers support for that operating system. Because of this, it is an excellent option for businesses that already utilise Juniper Networks as their infrastructure provider.

Simple API

PyEZ offers a straightforward and user-friendly application programming interface (API) for interacting with Junos OS. Because of this, it is much simpler for network engineers to begin automating their networks without having to first become proficient in a variety of difficult programming languages or frameworks.

Configurable

The architecture of PyEZ was built with configurability and extensibility in mind from the start. Because of this, organisations are able to tailor the library to meet their particular requirements, such as developing bespoke events or tables.

Cross-platform

PyEZ is a cross-platform library, which means that it is compatible with a wide variety of operating systems, such as Windows, Linux, and macOS. Because of this, it is an excellent option for businesses that operate in a network environment that is highly diverse.

Multiple Protocols

PyEZ is able to interact with Junos OS using a variety of protocols, including NETCONF, XML API, and SSH. This feature is made possible by PyEZ's support for multiple protocols. As a result, it is now feasible to automate tasks by making use of the protocol that is most suited to the particular use case.

In a nutshell, PyEZ is a Python library that, when installed on Juniper Networks devices running Junos OS, makes network automation more straightforward. Because its architecture is intended to be both customizable and extensible, it is an excellent option for businesses that need to automate their complex networks and has been designed to do so. PyEZ is an important tool for network automation tasks in environments that use Juniper Networks because of how easy it is to use, the options it provides for customization, and the support it provides for multiple protocols.

Configure nornir, paramiko, netmiko and pyEZ

Installing and Configuring Nornir

To configure Nornir, we need to install the Nornir library and create an inventory file that contains the details of the devices we want to automate.

Following are the steps:

- Install Nornir using pip:

```
pip install nornir
```

- Create an inventory file in YAML format. The inventory file should contain the hostname, IP address, and any other details required to connect to the device. Following is an example:

```
---
hosts:
  router1:
    hostname: 192.168.1.1
    platform: ios
    groups:
      - routers
  switch1:
    hostname: 192.168.1.2
    platform: ios
    groups:
      - switches
```

- Create a Python file that imports Nornir and runs an automation task. Following is an example:

```
from nornir import InitNornir

nr = InitNornir(config_file="config.yaml")

def my_task(task):
```

```
    # Code for the automation task goes here
    pass

results = nr.run(task=my_task)
```

Installing and Configuring Paramiko

To configure Paramiko, we need to install the Paramiko library and create a Python script that uses Paramiko to connect to a network device.

Following are the steps:

- Install Paramiko using pip:

```
pip install paramiko
```

- Create a Python script that imports Paramiko and connects to a network device using SSH. Following is an example:

```
import paramiko

ssh = paramiko.SSHClient()
ssh.set_missing_host_key_policy(paramiko.AutoAddPolicy())
ssh.connect('192.168.1.1', username='username', password='password')

stdin, stdout, stderr = ssh.exec_command('show version')

output = stdout.read().decode('utf-8')
print(output)

ssh.close()
```

Installing and Configuring Netmiko

To configure Netmiko, we need to install the Netmiko library and create a Python script that uses Netmiko to connect to a network device.

Following are the steps:

- Install Netmiko using pip:

```
pip install netmiko
```

- Create a Python script that imports Netmiko and connects to a network device using SSH. Following is an example:

```
from netmiko import ConnectHandler

device = {
  'device_type': 'cisco_ios',
  'ip': '192.168.1.1',
  'username': 'username',
  'password': 'password'
}

ssh = ConnectHandler(**device)

output = ssh.send_command('show version')

print(output)

ssh.disconnect()
```

Installing and Configuring PyEZ

To configure PyEZ, we need to install the Juniper PyEZ library and create a Python script that uses PyEZ to connect to a Junos device.

Following are the steps:

- Install PyEZ using pip:

```
pip install junos-eznc
```

- Create a Python script that imports PyEZ and connects to a Junos device using NETCONF. Following is an example:

```
from jnpr.junos import Device
from jnpr.junos.utils.config import Config

device = Device(host='192.168.1.1', user='username', password='password')
```

```
device.open()

config = Config(device)
config.lock()

config.load('set system host-name myrouter', format='set')
config.commit()

config.unlock()
device.close()
```

Overall, configuring Nornir, Paramiko, Netmiko, and PyEZ for network automation involves installing the required libraries and creating Python scripts that use these libraries to connect to network devices and perform automation tasks. Once these libraries are properly configured, network engineers can automate repetitive and time-consuming network tasks, improving network efficiency and reducing the risk of errors.

Configure Ports

It is the responsibility of network engineers to ensure that all network devices, such as routers and switches, are correctly configured so that they can facilitate communication between different devices that are connected to the same network. The configuration of ports on these devices is an essential part of a network engineer's job and is one of their primary responsibilities. The act of connecting a device to a network is the responsibility of a port, which is also referred to as an interface. It is possible to implement it either physically, such as with an Ethernet port, or logically, such as with a virtual interface. Both methods are valid.

It is typical for a network engineer to have to go through a series of steps before successfully configuring a port. These steps can differ depending on the particular device and the vendor, but some of the most common steps are as follows:

- The first thing that must be done in order to configure a port is to locate the port in question and determine what changes need to be made to it. Finding the physical location of the port on the device or determining the logical interface that needs to be configured may be required to accomplish this task.
- Once the port has been identified, the network engineer will typically adjust the settings for the port's speed and duplex. These adjustments are typically made after the network engineer has finished identifying the port. These settings determine whether the port communicates in a half-duplex or full-duplex mode,

as well as the maximum data transfer speed that can be achieved when sending and receiving data through the port.

- The process of configuring VLAN membership is supported by a wide variety of network devices. Virtual Local Area Networks (VLANs) are used to divide the network into logical groups and can be configured by the user. It is possible that the network engineer will have to configure the port so that it is a member of a specific VLAN.
- Access control lists (ACLs) are used to control which devices on a network can communicate with each other. These lists are used to determine which devices can communicate with each other. It's possible that the network engineer will need to configure ACLs on the port in order to restrict or allow traffic depending on the situation.
- Quality of Service (QoS) settings are used to give certain types of network traffic, like voice or video traffic, higher priority than other types of network traffic on the network. It's possible that the network engineer will have to configure the QoS settings on the port in order to make sure that the most important traffic gets priority over the less important traffic.
- Once the port has been configured, the network engineer will typically test the configuration to ensure that it is functioning as expected once it has been applied. In order to accomplish this, you may need to send test traffic through the port and then monitor the results.

It's possible that different kinds of network devices, like routers and switches, have a variety of port configurations available to them. Additionally, the configuration options that are available may vary depending on the vendor. However, a network engineer can normally configure a port so that it satisfies the requirements of the network and ensures that devices can communicate with one another in a dependable manner if they follow the steps outlined above.

Configuring Ports on Switches

Switches are the types of devices that are used in local area networks (LANs) and are responsible for connecting multiple devices to one another. Devices on the network are able to communicate with one another thanks to these switches, which serve as the network's "central hub."

During the process of configuring ports on switches, there are multiple steps that must be taken to ensure that the switch is configured correctly and optimised for the requirements of the network. When configuring ports on switches, the following steps are typically taken in most cases:

- Get in touch with the CLI (Command-Line Interface) (CLI): Accessing the switch's command-line interface is the very first thing to do when configuring a switch's ports (CLI). This can be accomplished in a number of different ways, such as by using the console, establishing a remote connection through Telnet or SSH, or utilising the web interface.
- Find out which port it is: After gaining access to the CLI, the next step is to locate the port that requires configuration and perform those settings. Either the port's name or its number can be used to accomplish this task. Take Cisco switches as an example; the names of their ports are typically formatted as follows: FastEthernet, GigabitEthernet, or TenGigabitEthernet, followed by the port number.
- Adjust the Velocity and the Duplex Mode: Following the successful identification of the port, the next step is to use the "speed" and "duplex" commands, respectively, to configure the port's speed and duplex mode. The speed of the port, which is typically measured in megabits per second (Mbps) or gigabits per second, can be changed with the help of the speed command (Gbps). It is possible to set the port's duplex mode using the duplex command. The port's duplex mode can be set to either full-duplex or half-duplex.

Administrators of a network are able to optimise a switch to meet the particular requirements of the network by configuring the speed and duplex mode of each port on the switch. For instance, if the network calls for the transfer of data at a high rate, the port's speed can be increased to a higher value, such as 10 gigabits per second (Gbps). In addition, if the network requires connections with low latency and high bandwidth, the full-duplex mode can be enabled to permit simultaneous transmission and reception of data. This is possible when the mode is enabled.

Let us look at the below example:

```
switch(config)# interface gigabitethernet 0/1
switch(config-if)# speed 1000
switch(config-if)# duplex full
```

- Configure VLAN membership for the port using the "switchport mode" and "switchport access vlan" commands. Let us look at the below example:

```
switch(config)# interface gigabitethernet 0/1
switch(config-if)# switchport mode access
switch(config-if)# switchport access vlan 10
```

- Configure ACLs to control traffic flowing through the port using the "ip access-group" command. Let us look at the below example:

```
switch(config)# access-list 100 permit tcp any any eq 80
switch(config)# interface gigabitethernet 0/1
switch(config-if)# ip access-group 100 in
```

Configuring Ports on Routers

Routers are devices in a network that perform the function of a gateway between two or more distinct networks. They are responsible for directing traffic between the various networks they are connected to and are used to connect multiple devices that belong to different networks.

The essential task of configuring the ports on routers is what enables network administrators to manage the flow of traffic through the network. This involves several steps, which are broken down into the following categories:

- Access the CLI of the router: It is necessary for network administrators to access the router's Command Line Interface in order to configure the ports on the router (CLI). This can either be accomplished through a direct connection to the console or through a remote connection using protocols like Telnet or SSH, or through the use of a web interface. Administrators are granted the ability to interact directly with the router's configuration settings when they have access to the CLI.
- Identify the port that needs to be configured: After gaining access to the CLI, the next step is to locate the port that requires configuration and perform those settings. In the majority of routers, ports can either be named or numbered to identify them. For instance, the names of the ports on Cisco routers begin with either FastEthernet, GigabitEthernet, or TenGigabitEthernet, and are then followed by the port number.

Identifying the port that needs to be configured is the first step in the process of configuring its speed and duplex mode. After that, the next step is to configure the port's speed. The commands "speed" and "duplex" are used to accomplish this goal. The "speed" command is used to set the rate at which data is transmitted on the port, whereas the "duplex" command is used to set the mode in which the port operates in duplex mode. Either "half-duplex" or "full-duplex" can be used to describe the duplex mode. In full-duplex mode, data can be transmitted in both directions at the same time, whereas in half-duplex mode, data can only be transmitted in one direction at a time in this mode.

When the port speed and duplex mode have been properly configured, the router will be in a better position to effectively manage the flow of traffic through the network. This may help to improve network performance and reduce the likelihood of network congestion occurring.

Let us look at the below example:

```
router(config)# interface gigabitethernet 0/1
router(config-if)# speed 1000
router(config-if)# duplex full
```

- Configure IP addresses on the port using the "ip address" command. Let us look at the below example:

```
router(config)# interface gigabitethernet 0/1
router(config-if)# ip address 192.168.1.1 255.255.255.0
```

Configure routing protocols for the port using the "router" command. Let us look at the below example:

```
router(config)# router ospf 1
router(config-router)# network 192.168.1.0 0.0.0.255 area 0
```

Accessing the device's command line interface (CLI), locating the port that needs to be configured, and configuring various parameters including speed, duplex, VLAN membership, access control lists, and routing protocols are the steps that make up the process of configuring ports on network devices. These configurations are unique to the vendor, and they can change depending on the device in use and the version of software installed. For more detailed instructions, network engineers should either consult the device's documentation or get in touch with the manufacturer.

Configure Hosts

In order to successfully set up a network, one of the most important steps is to configure the hosts on the network. Assigning IP addresses, subnet masks, and default gateways to each host is a necessary step in the process. Because the network is configured in this manner, hosts are able to communicate with other devices on the network and access the internet.

IP addresses are one-of-a-kind identifiers that are given to every device that is connected to a network. It makes it possible for different devices to communicate with one another over a network. The subnet mask both establishes the overall size of the network as well as partitions it into several more manageable sub-networks. The IP address of the router that is used to connect a local area network to the wider internet is known as the default gateway.

The process of configuring hosts differs from one operating system to another and also depends on the configuration of the network. The following are some of the most common steps for configuring hosts on operating systems running Windows and Linux:

Configuring Hosts on Windows

Configuring hosts on Windows is an important task that is essential for network connectivity. A host is a computer or device that is connected to a network, and its IP address is used to identify and communicate with other devices on the same network.

The process of configuring hosts on Windows involves several steps, which are outlined below:

- Step 1: Open the Control Panel and select "Network and Sharing Center". The first step in configuring hosts on Windows is to open the Control Panel and select "Network and Sharing Center." The Control Panel is a central location in Windows where users can configure and manage various settings on their computer. The Network and Sharing Center is a tool in Windows that provides an overview of network connections and enables users to manage network-related settings.
- Step 2: Click on "Change adapter settings" on the left-hand side of the screen. After opening the Network and Sharing Center, the next step is to click on "Change adapter settings" on the left-hand side of the screen. This will display a list of network adapters that are installed on the computer.
- Step 3: Right-click on the network adapter to be configured and select "Properties". Once the list of network adapters is displayed, the user should right-click on the network adapter that they wish to configure and select "Properties." This will display the properties dialog box for the selected network adapter.
- Step 4: Double-click on "Internet Protocol Version 4 (TCP/IPv4)" in the list of network protocols. In the properties dialog box for the selected network adapter, the user should double-click on "Internet Protocol Version 4 (TCP/IPv4)" in the list of network protocols. This will display the properties dialog box for the IPv4 protocol.
- Step 5: Select "Use the following IP address" and enter the IP address, subnet mask, and default gateway for the host. In the properties dialog box for the IPv4

protocol, the user should select "Use the following IP address" and enter the IP address, subnet mask, and default gateway for the host. The IP address is a unique identifier for the host on the network, and the subnet mask defines the network portion and the host portion of the IP address. The default gateway is the IP address of the router or gateway that is used to connect to other networks.

- Step 6: Click "OK" to save the configuration. Finally, the user should click "OK" to save the configuration. Once the configuration is saved, the host will be able to communicate with other devices on the network using the specified IP address and network settings.

In summary, configuring hosts on Windows involves opening the Control Panel, selecting "Network and Sharing Center," clicking on "Change adapter settings," right-clicking on the network adapter to be configured and selecting "Properties," double-clicking on "Internet Protocol Version 4 (TCP/IPv4)" in the list of network protocols, selecting "Use the following IP address" and entering the IP address, subnet mask, and default gateway for the host, and clicking "OK" to save the configuration.

Configuring Hosts on Linux

Configuring hosts on Linux involves setting up network connectivity on a computer or device running the Linux operating system. The process of configuring hosts on Linux can vary depending on the specific Linux distribution being used, but the general steps involved are as follows:

- The first step in configuring hosts on Linux is to open a terminal and log in as the root user. The root user has administrative privileges and can perform system-level tasks, such as configuring network interfaces.
- The next step is to locate and edit the network interface configuration file for the host. The location of this file can vary depending on the Linux distribution being used. For example, in Ubuntu, the file is located at /etc/network/interfaces.
- To edit the configuration file, you can use a text editor such as vi or nano. For example, to edit the file using nano, you can run the following command:

```
sudo nano /etc/network/interfaces
```

- This will open the configuration file in the nano text editor. Add the following lines to the configuration file:

```
auto eth0
iface eth0 inet static
address 192.168.1.100
```

```
netmask 255.255.255.0
gateway 192.168.1.1
```

- Save the configuration file and exit.
- Restart the networking service to apply the changes. The command to restart the networking service varies depending on the Linux distribution. For example, in Ubuntu, the command is:

```
sudo service networking restart
```

To provide a brief overview, the process of configuring hosts on a network involves giving each host an IP address, a subnet mask, and a default gateway. The configuration of hosts can change depending not only on the operating system but also on the configuration of the network. When attempting to correctly configure hosts, network engineers should first consult the documentation provided by both the operating system and the network.

Configure Servers

Configuring servers involves several steps, including installing the server operating system, configuring network settings, and installing and configuring server software.

Following are the general steps for configuring servers:

Installing Server Operating System

The first step in configuring a server is to install the server operating system. The steps involved in installing the server operating system vary depending on the server hardware and the operating system being used.

Configuring Network Settings

After installing the operating system, the next step is to configure the network settings. This includes assigning a static IP address, subnet mask, and default gateway. In addition, DNS servers may also need to be configured. The exact steps for configuring network settings depend on the server operating system being used.

Installing and Configuring Server Software

After configuring the network settings, the next step is to install and configure server software. The type of server software that needs to be installed depends on the purpose of the server. For example, a web server requires the installation of a web server software such as Apache or Nginx.

Following are the specific steps for configuring some commonly used servers:

Configuring a Web Server

Configuring a web server involves the following steps:

- Install a web server software such as Apache or Nginx.
- Configure the web server by editing the configuration files. This involves setting up the web server to serve content, defining virtual hosts, configuring SSL certificates, and setting up authentication and access control.
- Test the web server by accessing it from a web browser.

Configuring a File Server

Configuring a file server involves the following steps:

- Install file server software such as Samba or NFS.
- Configure the file server by editing the configuration files. This involves setting up the file server to share directories and files, defining access control, and configuring authentication.
- Test the file server by accessing it from a client computer.

Configuring a Database Server

Configuring a database server involves the following steps:

- Install database server software such as MySQL or PostgreSQL.
- Configure the database server by editing the configuration files. This involves setting up the database server to listen on the appropriate network interface, defining databases and tables, and configuring authentication and access control.
- Test the database server by accessing it from a client computer.

Therefore, configuring servers involves installing the server operating system, configuring network settings, and installing and configuring server software. The specific steps for configuring servers depend on the purpose of the server and the server software being used. Network engineers should consult the documentation for the server operating system and server software to configure servers correctly.

Configure Network Encryption

Configuring network encryption is an essential part of securing network communication. It involves encrypting data sent over the network to prevent unauthorized access to sensitive information.

There are several ways to configure network encryption, including the following:

SSL/TLS

SSL/TLS is a popular method for securing network communication. It works by encrypting data in transit using a certificate-based system. SSL/TLS requires the installation of a certificate on both the server and client. When a client connects to a server using SSL/TLS, the server sends its certificate to the client. The client verifies the certificate and establishes a secure connection with the server. All data transmitted between the client and server is encrypted using the SSL/TLS protocol.

To configure SSL/TLS, you will need to obtain and install a certificate on the server. This can be done using a certificate authority (CA) or a self-signed certificate. Once the certificate is installed, you will need to configure your server software to use SSL/TLS.

IPsec

IPsec is another method for securing network communication. It works by encrypting data at the IP layer of the network stack. IPsec requires the installation of a security policy on both the client and server. When a client connects to a server using IPsec, the client and server negotiate a security policy that defines how the data will be encrypted. All data transmitted between the client and server is encrypted using the security policy.

To configure IPsec, you will need to install and configure an IPsec implementation on both the client and server. IPsec implementations include strongSwan, OpenSwan, and LibreSwan.

SSH

SSH is a secure protocol used for remote access to servers. It works by encrypting data sent between the client and server using public key encryption. SSH requires the installation of an SSH server on the server and an SSH client on the client. When a client connects to a server using SSH, the client sends its public key to the server. The server verifies the public key and establishes a secure connection with the client. All data transmitted between the client and server is encrypted using SSH.
To configure SSH, you will need to install and configure an SSH server on the server and an SSH client on the client. SSH implementations include OpenSSH and PuTTY.

VPN

VPN is a method for securing network communication by creating a secure tunnel between the client and server. VPN requires the installation of VPN software on both the client and server. When a client connects to a server using VPN, the client and server negotiate a secure tunnel through which all data is transmitted. All data transmitted between the client and server is encrypted using the VPN protocol.

To configure VPN, you will need to install and configure VPN software on both the client and server. VPN implementations include OpenVPN, Cisco AnyConnect, and Fortinet FortiClient.

To summarize, configuring network encryption involves encrypting data sent over the network to prevent unauthorized access to sensitive information. There are several methods for configuring network encryption, including SSL/TLS, IPsec, SSH, and VPN. Network engineers should choose the appropriate method for their network and configure it correctly to ensure the security of their network communication.

Testing the Network Automation Environment

Once you have set up your network automation lab and configured NS3 emulator, libraries like Nornir, Paramiko, Netmiko, and PyEZ, ports, hosts, and servers, you need to ensure that everything is working as expected.
There are several ways to test your network automation lab to verify that it is configured properly, including the following:

Test Connectivity between Hosts

The first step in testing network automation lab is to ensure that there is connectivity between all the hosts in the network. This is an important step as it lays the foundation for any further testing or automation tasks. The ping command is a useful tool for this purpose.

The ping command is a utility that sends a small packet of data to a destination host and waits for a response. The command can be run from the command line interface of any host in the network. It is a simple yet effective way to test connectivity between hosts. To use the ping command, the user must specify the destination host's IP address or hostname. The command then sends an ICMP (Internet Control Message Protocol) echo request packet to the destination host. If the destination host receives the packet, it responds with an ICMP echo reply packet. The time taken for the packet to travel to the destination host and back is measured and displayed as the round trip time (RTT).

If the host responds with an ICMP echo reply packet, it indicates that connectivity is working properly between the two hosts. If the host does not respond, it may indicate a problem with the network configuration. In addition to testing connectivity between hosts, the ping command can also be used to test other aspects of the network. For example, it can be used to test the network's response time or to troubleshoot network issues such as packet loss or high latency.

Ping is a commonly used tool in network troubleshooting and testing. It is a simple yet effective way to verify connectivity and can help to identify network issues. It is also a valuable tool for network automation, as it can be used to automate network testing tasks and ensure that the network is functioning properly.

To test connectivity between hosts, you can use the following command:

```
ping <ip address or hostname>
```

For example, if you want to test connectivity between host1 and host2, you can use the following command:

```
ping host2
```

Test Port Connectivity

After verifying that there is network connectivity between hosts, the next step is to test port connectivity. Port connectivity tests whether a specific port on a remote host is open and accepting connections. This is an important step in troubleshooting network connectivity issues or verifying that a service is running on a particular port.

There are different ways to test port connectivity, but two common methods are telnet and netcat.

The telnet command is a client-server protocol that connects to a remote host on a specific port and displays any response from the server. The telnet command is available on most operating systems and can be used to test port connectivity on a remote host. To use the telnet command, you need to know the IP address or hostname of the remote host and the port number you want to connect to. For example, to test if port 80 is open on a web server with IP address 192.168.0.1, you would use the following command:

```
telnet 192.168.0.1 80
```

If the port is open and accepting connections, you should see a response from the server indicating that the connection was successful. If the port is closed or not accepting connections, you will receive an error message.

The netcat command is another tool that can be used to test port connectivity. Unlike telnet, netcat allows you to send and receive data over the network. The netcat command is available on Linux and other Unix-like operating systems. To use netcat, you need to know the IP address or hostname of the remote host and the port number you want to connect to. For example, to test if port 22 is open on a remote server with IP address 192.168.0.2, you would use the following command:

```
nc -vz 192.168.0.2 22
```

The -v option makes the output more verbose, and the -z option makes netcat scan for listening daemons, without sending any data. The output of this command will indicate whether the port is open or not.

To test port connectivity using the telnet command, use the following command:

```
telnet <ip address or hostname> <port>
```

For example, if you want to test port 80 on host2, you can use the following command:

```
telnet host2 80
```

To test port connectivity using the netcat command, use the following command:

```
nc -vz <ip address or hostname> <port>
```

For example, if you want to test port 80 on host2, you can use the following command:

```
nc -vz host2 80
```

Test SSH Connectivity

SSH (Secure Shell) is a secure protocol used for remote login and other secure network services over an unsecured network. If you have configured SSH on your network, you can test SSH connectivity using the ssh command. The ssh command connects to a host using SSH and opens a shell on the remote host. This enables you to access the command-line interface of the remote host and execute commands as if you were physically present at the remote host.

To test SSH connectivity using the ssh command, you need to have SSH client software installed on your local computer. Most modern operating systems, including Linux, macOS, and Windows, have SSH client software pre-installed, but if not, you can install it easily.

To test SSH connectivity, use the following command:

```
ssh <username>@<ip address or hostname>
```

For example, if you want to test SSH connectivity to host2 as the user "user1", you can use the following command:

```
ssh user1@host2
```

Test Network Automation Libraries

To test your network automation libraries, you can write a simple script that performs a basic task, such as retrieving the interface configuration of a network device. You can use the library documentation to determine the correct syntax and commands to use.

For example, to test the PyEZ library, you can write a script that retrieves the interface configuration of a Juniper device. The script might look something like this:

```
from jnpr.junos import Device

dev = Device(host=<ip address or hostname>, user=<username>,
password=<password>)
dev.open()

interfaces = dev.rpc.get_interface_information()
print(interfaces)

dev.close()
```

Test NS3 Emulator

To test the NS3 emulator, you can create a simple network topology and run a simulation. You can use the NS3 documentation to determine the correct syntax and commands to use.
For example, to test the NS3 emulator, you can create a simple network topology with two nodes connected by a point-to-point link.

The topology might look something like this:

```
# Import NS3 modules
import ns.applications
import ns.core
import ns.internet
import ns.network
```

```
# Create nodes
node1 = ns.network.Node()
node2 = ns.network.Node()
```

```
# Create point-to-point link
pointToPoint = ns.network.PointToPointHelper()
pointToPoint.SetDeviceAttribute("DataRate", ns.core.StringValue("5Mbps"))
pointToPoint.SetChannelAttribute("Delay", ns.core.StringValue("2ms"))
```

```
# Create network interfaces
device1 = pointToPoint.Install(node1)
device2 = pointToPoint.Install(node2)

address1 = ns.internet.Ipv4AddressHelper()
address1.SetBase(ns.network.Ipv4Address("10.1.1.0"),
ns.network.Ipv4Mask("255.255.255.0"))

address2 = ns.internet.Ipv4AddressHelper()
address2.SetBase(ns.network.Ipv4Address("10.1.2.0"),
ns.network.Ipv4Mask("255.255.255.0"))
```

```
# Assign IP addresses to interfaces
interface1 = address1.Assign(device1)
interface2 = address2.Assign(device2)
```

```
# Create TCP sender and receiver applications
packetSinkHelper =
ns.applications.PacketSinkHelper("ns3::TcpSocketFactory",
ns.network.InetSocketAddress(ns.network.Ipv4Address.GetAny(), 9))
sink = packetSinkHelper.Install(node2)

onOffHelper = ns.applications.OnOffHelper("ns3::TcpSocketFactory",
ns.network.InetSocketAddress(interface2.GetAddress(0), 9))
onOffHelper.SetAttribute("OnTime",
ns.core.StringValue("ns3::ConstantRandomVariable[Constant=1]"))
onOffHelper.SetAttribute("OffTime",
ns.core.StringValue("ns3::ConstantRandomVariable[Constant=0]"))
onOffHelper.SetAttribute("DataRate",
ns.network.DataRateValue(ns.network.DataRate("5Mbps")))
onOffHelper.SetAttribute("PacketSize", ns.core.UintegerValue(1000))

source = onOffHelper.Install(node1)
```

```
# Create simulation object and run
simulator = ns.core.Simulator()
simulator.Schedule(ns.core.Seconds(1.0), &source.Start)
simulator.Schedule(ns.core.Seconds(10.0), &source.Stop)

simulator.Run()
```

This script creates a point-to-point link between two nodes, assigns IP addresses to the interfaces, and creates TCP sender and receiver applications. The simulation runs for 10 seconds and then stops.

Test Network Encryption

You can put the security of your network to the test by capturing and examining network traffic with the help of the Wireshark network analyzer tool. If you know the key or passphrase, you can use Wireshark to decrypt traffic that is encrypted. Run a network application on the network that makes use of encryption, such as SSH or HTTPS, and then use Wireshark to record the traffic generated by the application. This will allow you to test network encryption. After that, you'll be able to conduct an investigation into the traffic to ensure that the encrypted data is hidden from view.

Testing your network automation lab is a crucial step in making certain that everything is operating as it should be. You are able to test connectivity between hosts, connectivity between ports, connectivity between SSH, network automation libraries, connectivity with the NS3 emulator, and encryption on the network. You will be able to pinpoint any configuration problems with your network automation lab if you test each individual component of the lab. This will also ensure that the lab is set up correctly to meet your requirements.

Summary

In this chapter, we discussed about the components required for setting up a network automation lab, including libraries such as Nornir, Paramiko, Netmiko, and PyEZ, as well as virtual machines and network devices. We discussed the process of configuring ports, hosts, and servers in the network automation lab. This involved defining network topologies, assigning IP addresses, and configuring applications such as TCP sender and receiver.

Finally, we talked about the importance of testing the network automation lab to ensure that it is working properly. This involved testing connectivity between hosts, port connectivity, SSH connectivity, network automation libraries, NS3 emulator, and network encryption. We also discussed using tools such as Wireshark to capture and analyze network traffic to test network encryption. Overall, setting up a network automation lab can be a complex process, but it offers numerous benefits for network management. By following the steps outlined in this chapter and testing the lab properly, you can ensure that your lab is configured properly and working as expected.

Chapter 5: Code, Test & Validate Network Automation

Understanding Network Automation Scripts

Network automation scripts are scripts that automate tasks in a network environment, such as configuring network devices, monitoring network traffic, or managing network security. Python is a popular language for network automation due to its simplicity, readability, and extensive libraries for network automation. In this chapter, we will describe the concepts involved in creating network automation scripts using Python.

One of the main concepts involved in network automation scripts is the use of APIs. In the context of network automation, APIs are used to interact with network devices, such as routers and switches, and perform tasks such as configuring interfaces or retrieving device information. APIs can be used to communicate with devices using various protocols, such as SNMP (Simple Network Management Protocol) or NETCONF (Network Configuration Protocol).

Another key concept involved in network automation scripts is the use of libraries. Python has several libraries for network automation, as discussed in the previous chapter, which provide pre-built functions and tools for interacting with network devices and protocols. These libraries can simplify the task of creating network automation scripts and reduce the amount of code needed to perform complex tasks.

In addition to APIs and libraries, network automation scripts also rely on data structures and algorithms. Data structures, such as dictionaries or lists, are used to organize and store data, such as device information or configuration data. Algorithms, such as search or sorting algorithms, can be used to perform complex tasks, such as finding a specific device in a network or analyzing network traffic.

Error handling is another important concept in network automation scripts. As with any software, network automation scripts can encounter errors, such as network connectivity issues or incorrect configuration data. To handle these errors, scripts can use exception handling, which allows the script to continue running even if an error occurs. Exception handling can also provide feedback to the user, such as logging the error message or sending an email notification.

Finally, network automation scripts may also use database systems to store and retrieve network data. Database systems, such as MySQL or PostgreSQL, can be used to store device configuration data, network topology information, or network traffic data. These databases can be accessed using SQL (Structured Query Language) queries, which can be executed from within a Python script.

To summarize, network automation scripts using Python rely on APIs, libraries, data structures, and algorithms to automate tasks in a network environment. Exception handling and database systems are also important concepts in network automation scripts. By leveraging these concepts, network automation scripts can simplify the task of managing a network environment and improve the efficiency and accuracy of network management tasks.

Procedure of Network Automation Scripts

Following are the steps involved in writing, testing, and validating network automation scripts in Python:

- Determine the Task: The first thing you need to do is figure out the task that you want the script to take care of for you. Performing tasks such as configuring network devices or monitoring network traffic could fall into this category.
- Pick a Public Library: Pick a library that offers all of the features and resources that are required for the task at hand. If you want to automate the configuration of network devices, for instance, you could go with the Netmiko library.
- Bring in the Collection: Utilizing the "import" statement, bring the desired library into the Python script you're working on.
- Specify the Variables: Define the variables that will hold the required data, such as IP addresses or configuration data, and then use those variables to store the data.
- Create the Code: Create the code that, when run, will carry out the required actions by making use of the functions and tools provided by the library.
- Put the Code to the Test: Run the code through its paces by putting it through its paces in a test environment or on test devices to ensure that it performs as anticipated.
- Debugging the Code: When testing is complete, you should debug any errors or problems that were discovered. This may involve using print statements to check the values of variables or using a debugger tool to step through the code. Both of these options are possible.
- Validate the Code: Validate the code by executing it on devices or in an environment that is intended for production. This step is essential for ensuring that the code is functioning appropriately and will not result in any problems when it is deployed in a production setting.
- Documenting the Code: To document the code, add comments that explain the purpose of each section of code and the variables that are being used. Because of this, it will be simpler for others to understand the code in the future and make modifications to it.
- Version Control: Make use of tools for version control, such as Git, in order to keep track of changes that have been made to the code and collaborate with other members of your team.

Determining the task, selecting a library, defining variables, writing the code, testing the code, debugging any issues that arise, validating the code on production devices, documenting the code, and using version control tools to manage changes to the code are all components of the process of writing, testing, and validating network automation scripts in Python. If you follow these steps, you will increase the likelihood that the script will automate network tasks in a way that is effective, efficient, and reliable.

Define Variables for Automation Scripts

Defining variables in Python is a critical step when writing network automation scripts. In this sample program illustration, we will show you how to define variables in Python by writing a simple script that automates the process of configuring a network device.

Install Required Libraries

Before writing the script, we need to make sure that we have the necessary libraries installed. In the below code, we will be using the Netmiko library, which we can install using the following command:

```
pip install netmiko
```

Import Libraries

Next, we need to import the necessary libraries into our Python script using the import statement. In the below code, we will import the netmiko library.

```
import netmiko
```

Define Variables

Now that we have the necessary libraries imported, we can define the variables that we will use in our script.

In the below code, we will define the following variables:

- device_type: The type of network device we want to configure, such as Cisco IOS, Cisco Nexus, or Juniper Junos.
- ip_address: The IP address of the device we want to configure.
- username: The username we will use to authenticate with the device.
- password: The password we will use to authenticate with the device.
- config_commands: The configuration commands we want to send to the device.

Following is the code that defines these variables:

```
device_type = 'cisco_ios'
ip_address = '192.168.1.1'
username = 'admin'
password = 'password'
config_commands = ['interface GigabitEthernet0/0', 'ip address 192.168.2.1
255.255.255.0', 'no shutdown']
```

Connect to Device

With our variables defined, we can now connect to the network device using the ConnectHandler() method from the Netmiko library. This method takes the following parameters: device_type, ip_address, username, and password.

```
device = {
    'device_type': device_type,
    'ip': ip_address,
    'username': username,
    'password': password
}

net_connect = netmiko.ConnectHandler(**device)
```

Send Configuration Commands

With our connection established, we can now send the configuration commands to the device using the send_config_set() method from the Netmiko library. This method takes a list of configuration commands as its parameter.

```
output = net_connect.send_config_set(config_commands)
print(output)
```

Close Connection

Once we have sent the configuration commands, we should close the connection to the device to free up resources.

```
net_connect.disconnect()
```

Putting all of these steps together, below is the complete Python script that defines variables and uses the Netmiko library to configure a network device:

```
import netmiko

device_type = 'cisco_ios'
ip_address = '192.168.1.1'
username = 'admin'
password = 'password'
config_commands = ['interface GigabitEthernet0/0', 'ip address 192.168.2.1
255.255.255.0', 'no shutdown']

device = {
  'device_type': device_type,
  'ip': ip_address,
  'username': username,
  'password': password
}

net_connect = netmiko.ConnectHandler(**device)

output = net_connect.send_config_set(config_commands)
print(output)

net_connect.disconnect()
```

Create Script to Use Variables

Now, we can use the variables that we have defined in our Python script. Following is an example of how to use the variables that we have defined:

```
#!/usr/bin/env python
# Define variables
device_type = 'cisco_ios'
ip_address = '10.0.0.1'
username = 'admin'
```

```
password = 'password'

# Use variables
print('Connecting to device at {}:'.format(ip_address))
print('Device type: {}'.format(device_type))
print('Username: {}'.format(username))
print('Password: {}'.format(password))
```

In this script, we have defined the variables device_type, ip_address, username, and password. We then used these variables in the print() statements to display the device information.

Run the Script

To run the script, save the code into a file with the .py extension and execute it from the terminal or command prompt.

```
$ python script_name.py
```

When the script is executed, it will display the device information that we defined in the variables.

```
Connecting to device at 10.0.0.1:
Device type: cisco_ios
Username: admin
Password: password
```

By following these steps, we can define variables in our Python scripts for network automation and use them to simplify our code and make it more flexible.

Write Codes using Python Tools

Following is a sample demonstration to write code for network automation tasks using Python libraries and tools:

Install Required Libraries and Tools

Before we start writing our code, we need to make sure that we have the necessary libraries and tools installed. For network automation, we can use libraries such as Nornir, Paramiko, Netmiko, and PyEZ.

To install these libraries, we can use the pip command in the terminal or command prompt:

```
pip install nornir paramiko netmiko junos-eznc
```

Import Libraries

Once we have installed the necessary libraries, we need to import them into our Python script. Following is an example of how to import these libraries:

```
from nornir import InitNornir
from nornir.plugins.tasks.networking import netmiko_send_command
from nornir.plugins.tasks.networking import napalm_get
from nornir.plugins.functions.text import print_result
from paramiko import SSHClient
from paramiko import AutoAddPolicy
from junos import Junos_Context
```

In this script, we are importing the Nornir library, which is a Python automation framework that simplifies network automation tasks. We are also importing the netmiko_send_command and napalm_get tasks from the Nornir networking plugin, which allows us to run commands on network devices. We are using the print_result function to print the output of our commands. Additionally, we are importing the Paramiko SSH client, which allows us to connect to network devices over SSH. Finally, we are importing the Junos Context from PyEZ library, which provides context information for Juniper devices.

Define Inventory

The Nornir framework uses an inventory to manage devices and groups of devices. We need to define the inventory in our script before we can use it.

Following is an example of how to define the inventory:

```
nr = InitNornir(
  inventory={
     "plugin": "SimpleInventory",
     "options": {
        "host_file": "hosts.yaml",
```

```
        "group_file": "groups.yaml",
    },
  }
)
```

In this script, we are using the InitNornir function to initialize Nornir with a SimpleInventory plugin. We are specifying the location of our host and group files in the options parameter.

Define Tasks

We need to define the tasks that we want to perform on our devices. Following is an example of how to define a task that retrieves the running configuration of a device using Netmiko:

```
def get_config(task):
  result = task.run(
    task=netmiko_send_command,
    command_string="show running-config",
  )
  task.host["config"] = result.result
```

In this script, we define a function called get_config that takes a task as an argument. We use the netmiko_send_command task to retrieve the running configuration of the device and store it in the config attribute of the host object.

Define Playbook

Finally, we need to define the playbook that combines the tasks and devices that we want to run them on. Following is an example of how to define a playbook that runs the get_config task on all devices in our inventory:

```
from nornir.core.filter import F

def main():
  ios = nr.filter(F(platform="ios"))
  results = ios.run(task=get_config)
  print_result(results)
```

In this script, we define a function called main that filters the devices in our inventory that are running IOS. We then run the get_config task on those devices and print

Execute the Script

Once the script has been written and saved, it can be executed using the command:

```
python script_name.py
```

This will run the script and perform the network automation tasks that were defined in the script. The output of the script can be viewed in the console.

Test and Validate the Script

After the script has been executed, it is important to test and validate the results to ensure that the network automation tasks were performed correctly. This can be done by manually verifying the changes made by the script, or by using additional scripts to gather information about the network and compare it to the desired state.

Following is an example script that demonstrates the process of defining variables, importing libraries, and performing network automation tasks using Python:

```
import paramiko

# Define Variables
ip_address = "10.0.0.1"
username = "admin"
password = "password"
command = "show interfaces"

# Establish SSH Connection
ssh = paramiko.SSHClient()
ssh.set_missing_host_key_policy(paramiko.AutoAddPolicy())
ssh.connect(ip_address, username=username, password=password)

# Send Command
stdin, stdout, stderr = ssh.exec_command(command)

# Print Output
```

```
print(stdout.read().decode())

# Close Connection
ssh.close()
```

In this script, the paramiko library is imported and used to establish an SSH connection to a network device with the specified IP address, username, and password. The command variable is defined to specify the command that will be sent to the device. The exec_command() method is used to send the command to the device, and the output is printed to the console using the print() function. Finally, the SSH connection is closed using the close() method.

To run this script, save it as a .py file and execute it using the command:

```
python script_name.py
```

This will establish an SSH connection to the device, send the specified command, and print the output to the console.

To conclude, network automation using Python involves defining variables, importing libraries, writing code to perform network automation tasks, and testing and validating the results. By following these steps and using the available tools and libraries, network engineers can automate repetitive tasks, improve efficiency, and reduce errors in network management.

Testing Network Automation Scripts

During the development process, one of the most important steps is testing the code for the network automation. This step ensures that the code will carry out the desired tasks and will function correctly and without errors. When it comes to automating network tasks, this is of utmost importance because errors in the code could potentially cause issues with network connectivity and compromise security.

Creating a test environment or utilising test devices is the initial step in the process of testing code for network automation. A test environment is an environment that is distinct from the production environment. It is an environment that can be used to test new code changes without having an effect on the live network. Whether you choose to do it physically or virtually, you can accomplish this goal by constructing an exact copy of the production environment.

After the test environment has been prepared, the network automation code can be executed either on the test devices or within the test environment itself. It is necessary to conduct tests to determine whether or not the code is capable of carrying out the activities that are required, such as configuring devices, gathering data, and creating backups. In addition to that, the code ought to be examined for its capacity to deal with errors and exceptions.

In order to properly test the code for the network automation, it is essential to have a complete set of test cases that account for every conceivable circumstance. This includes both positive and negative test cases, which evaluate the capability of the code to respond appropriately to a variety of inputs and circumstances.

Test cases that are considered positive are those in which it is anticipated that the code will successfully complete a particular activity. A good example of a positive test case for configuring a switch would be to configure a VLAN and then check to see that the VLAN was successfully created after making the appropriate configuration changes. Test cases that are considered to be negative are those in which it is anticipated that the code will fail or generate an error. A negative test case for configuring a switch could consist of, for instance, configuring a VLAN that already exists and ensuring that the code generates an error message in response to the configuration.

During the testing phase, it is essential to make sure that errors and exceptions are checked for, in addition to monitoring the output of the code. Any problems that arise must be recorded and communicated, after which the code must be altered and retested until all of the problems have been fixed.

Set Up a Test Environment

Before testing the code, it is important to set up a test environment that closely mimics the production environment. This can include test devices, virtual machines, and test networks. The test environment should be isolated from the production environment to prevent any unintended consequences.

Create Test Cases

Test cases should be created to ensure that the code performs the desired tasks and handles errors appropriately.

Test cases can include scenarios such as:

- Successful execution of the code
- Incorrect input parameters
- Device connectivity issues
- Incorrect output from the code

Run the Code

Once the test environment and test cases have been set up, the code can be run to perform the network automation tasks. The output of the code should be compared to the expected output to ensure that the code is working as expected.

Following is an example code that demonstrates how to test network automation code by running it on a test device:

```
import paramiko

# Define Variables
ip_address = "10.0.0.1"
username = "admin"
password = "password"
command = "show interfaces"

# Establish SSH Connection
ssh = paramiko.SSHClient()
ssh.set_missing_host_key_policy(paramiko.AutoAddPolicy())
ssh.connect(ip_address, username=username, password=password)

# Send Command
stdin, stdout, stderr = ssh.exec_command(command)

# Validate Output
output = stdout.read().decode()
if "Interface" in output:
  print("Test Passed")
else:
  print("Test Failed")

# Close Connection
ssh.close()
```

In the above code, the code establishes an SSH connection to a test device and sends the command show interfaces. The output of the command is validated to ensure that it contains the string "Interface". If the output contains this string, the test is considered passed. If not, the test is considered failed.

Document Test Results

After running the code and validating the output, it is important to document the test results. This can include the date and time the test was performed, the test cases that were executed, and the results of each test case.

By following these steps, network automation code can be tested to ensure that it works as expected and performs the desired tasks without errors. Testing network automation code is a critical step in the development process and can help prevent errors from being introduced into the production environment.

Debug Errors

During the process of developing software, errors, bugs, and other problems may crop up. This process is known as "debugging," and it involves finding and fixing these problems. It is a crucial stage in the process of guaranteeing that the software in question functions properly and satisfies the needs of its end users. Debugging is an essential part of network automation because it ensures that scripts perform as intended and can respond appropriately to any errors or unexpected events that may arise. In this section, we will demonstrate how to debug errors or issues that arise during testing using Python.

Identify the Error or Issue

The first step in debugging is to identify the error or issue that is occurring. This can be done by reviewing the error message or output from the code.

Review the Code

Once the error or issue has been identified, the code should be reviewed to determine the cause of the error or issue. This can involve reviewing the syntax of the code, reviewing the input parameters, or reviewing the output of the code.

Use Print Statements

One effective way to debug code is to use print statements. Print statements can be used to output the values of variables or the status of the code at various points during execution.

```
# Define Variables
a = 10
b = 20

# Debug Code with Print Statements
print("Value of a: ", a)
print("Value of b: ", b)

c = a + b
print("Value of c: ", c)
```

In the above code, print statements are used to output the values of the variables a, b, and c at various points during execution. This can help identify the cause of errors or issues that are occurring.

Use a Debugger

Python also includes a built-in debugger that can be used to step through code line-by-line and identify errors or issues. The debugger can be launched by adding the following line of code to the script:

```
import pdb; pdb.set_trace()
```

This line of code will launch the debugger at the point where it is placed in the script. Once the debugger is launched, it can be used to step through the code line-by-line, view the values of variables, and identify errors or issues.

Fix the Error or Issue

Once the cause of the error or issue has been identified, the code can be modified to fix the error or issue. This can involve correcting syntax errors, modifying input parameters, or modifying the output of the code.

Test the Code

After the code has been modified, it should be tested again to ensure that the error or issue has been resolved. The code should be run on a test environment or test devices, and the output should be compared to the expected output.

By following these steps, errors or issues that arise during testing can be identified and resolved using Python. Debugging is an essential step in the software development process and can help ensure that network automation code works as expected and performs the desired tasks without errors.

Validate Network Automation Scripts

In the process of developing software, one of the most important steps is called "validating the code for network automation." This step is necessary because it ensures that the code will function as expected once it is deployed to the production environment. When network automation code is run on production devices, developers receive feedback on the functionality, performance, and reliability of their code based on how well it actually works in the real world.

In order to validate code for network automation, the first step is to perform in-depth testing of the code in a staging or test environment. This environment ought to be a copy of the production environment, complete with the production environment's network topology, devices, and configurations, and it ought to be a replica of the production environment. When the code is deployed to the production environment, this will help to ensure that it behaves as expected in the way that was intended.

It is possible to deploy the code to the production environment or devices after it has been validated in the staging or test environment. It is essential to perform a code review prior to deploying the code to the production environment. This review should ensure that the code is well-documented, that it complies with coding standards, and that it does not introduce any security vulnerabilities.

It is essential to carry out the code deployment in a controlled manner if you wish for it to be successful when applied to production devices. This can be accomplished through the use of methods such as phased deployment, in which the code is initially rolled out to a select group of devices, and then gradually rolled out to the entire production environment over the course of some time. Before the code is deployed to the entire production environment, any problems or bugs that may exist can therefore be located and fixed before the code is deployed. After deployment, it is essential to perform close monitoring of both the devices and the network in order to validate the network automation code. Using tools for network monitoring that are able to detect any issues or irregularities present in the network is one way to accomplish this goal. In order to maintain the reliability and safety of the network, it is imperative that any errors or problems that crop up be resolved as quickly as possible.

In addition to keeping an eye on the network, it is critical to validate the operation of the automation code for the network. Using test scripts that simulate a variety of different network conditions and verify that the code behaves as expected is one way to accomplish this goal. Any problems or errors that are found should be documented, addressed, and put through another round of testing to ensure that they have been fixed.

In this section, we will demonstrate how to validate network automation code by running it on the production environment or devices.

Prepare the Production Environment

Before running the network automation code on the production environment or devices, it is essential to ensure that the environment or devices are properly prepared. This can involve performing backups, verifying network connectivity, and verifying that the necessary software and libraries are installed.

Deploy Code to Production Environment or Devices

Once the production environment or devices are properly prepared, the network automation code can be deployed to the production environment or devices. This can be done using a variety of methods, including copying the code to the production environment or devices using SCP or SFTP.

```
# Copy Code to Production Environment or Devices
import paramiko

# Define SSH Connection
ssh = paramiko.SSHClient()
ssh.set_missing_host_key_policy(paramiko.AutoAddPolicy())
ssh.connect(hostname='prod-device', username='user', password='password')

# Copy Code to Device
sftp = ssh.open_sftp()
sftp.put('network_automation.py', '/home/user/network_automation.py')
```

```
sftp.close()
```

In the above code, the paramiko library is used to establish an SSH connection to the production device and copy the network_automation.py script to the device.

Run the Code on Production Environment or Devices

Once the code has been deployed to the production environment or devices, it can be executed using the Python interpreter.

```
# Execute Code on Production Environment or Devices
import paramiko

# Define SSH Connection
ssh = paramiko.SSHClient()
ssh.set_missing_host_key_policy(paramiko.AutoAddPolicy())
ssh.connect(hostname='prod-device', username='user', password='password')

# Execute Code on Device
stdin, stdout, stderr = ssh.exec_command('python
/home/user/network_automation.py')
output = stdout.readlines()
errors = stderr.readlines()

# Print Output and Errors
print("Output: ", output)
print("Errors: ", errors)

ssh.close()
```

In the above code, the paramiko library is used to establish an SSH connection to the production device and execute the network_automation.py script on the device.

Verify the Output

After the code has been executed on the production environment or devices, it is essential to verify the output to ensure that the code works correctly and without errors. This can involve reviewing the output to ensure that the expected tasks were performed and that no errors or issues were encountered.

By following these steps, network automation code can be validated by running it on the production environment or devices. Validating network automation code is essential to ensure that the code works as expected and without errors when deployed to the production environment.

Summary

In this chapter, we discussed the steps involved in writing, testing, and validating network automation scripts using Python. We delved into the steps involved in writing network automation scripts in Python. We started by defining the variables required for automation scripts, such as IP addresses, usernames, and passwords. We also explained how to use the appropriate libraries and tools for various tasks such as connecting to devices, configuring ports, hosts, and servers, and implementing network encryption.

After that, we discussed testing the network automation code by running it on a test environment or test devices to ensure that it is working as expected. We explained the importance of testing and debugging to identify and fix any errors or issues that arise during testing. We also demonstrated how to use Python's built-in debugging tools to locate and fix errors in the code. Finally, we discussed the validation of network automation code by running it on the production environment or devices. We explained the importance of testing on a production environment to ensure that the code works as intended and does not cause any unexpected issues.

To sum it up, writing, testing, and validating network automation scripts is a crucial aspect of network automation. By following the steps outlined in this chapter, network administrators can create effective and reliable automation scripts that can help them save time, increase productivity, and reduce errors in their network management tasks.

CHAPTER 6: AUTOMATION OF CONFIGURATION MANAGEMENT

Why Configuration Management?

Need of Configuration Management

The process of managing and keeping track of the configuration of hardware and software systems within a network environment is referred to as configuration management. It entails keeping track of changes made to systems, applications, and devices in order to guarantee that their configurations are accurate and consistent at all times.

Because it contributes to the preservation of the steadiness and uniformity of the network environment, configuration management is an essential component of contemporary IT infrastructure management. IT teams are able to quickly identify and troubleshoot issues when they track changes and configurations. This helps to minimise the impact that downtime has on network operations. The amount of time that network systems are unavailable can be cut down and their reliability can be improved thanks to configuration management.

The fact that configuration management guarantees that all systems and applications are configured in an accurate and consistent manner is one of the most important advantages it offers. When systems are not configured correctly, it is possible for errors, vulnerabilities, and conflicts to occur. This helps to avoid those issues. IT teams are able to improve the overall performance of the network environment if they take the precaution of ensuring that all of the systems are configured in the same manner. This lowers the risk of unexpected behaviour.

In addition to its other advantages, configuration management helps to increase the dependability of network systems while simultaneously decreasing the amount of downtime they experience. IT teams are able to quickly identify and troubleshoot issues that may arise thanks to the practise of tracking changes and configurations. This helps to minimise the impact that downtime has on network operations. In addition to this, configuration management helps to ensure that systems are properly updated and maintained, which in turn reduces the likelihood of failures occurring within the system.

In addition to being essential for compliance and security, configuration management is also very important. It helps ensure that all systems are configured in accordance with the standards and best practises of the industry, and that any security vulnerabilities are identified and addressed as quickly as possible. IT departments can benefit from the use of configuration management tools to better identify potential security flaws and monitor their level of compliance with industry standards and regulations.

Configuration management is an essential component of the management of modern information technology infrastructure. It helps to maintain the consistency and steadiness of the network environment, while also reducing downtime, increasing reliability, ensuring compliance, and enhancing security. IT teams are able to effectively manage and track the configuration of hardware and software systems by utilising the tools and processes that are associated with configuration management. This helps to ensure that the systems are configured correctly and consistently.

Role of Python in Configuration Management

Python is a high-level programming language that is frequently employed in the process of automating tasks related to configuration management. The process of managing the configuration of software, hardware, and network devices for the purpose of ensuring that they function in an effective and secure manner is referred to as configuration management.

Python's user-friendliness is one of the primary factors that contribute to its widespread adoption for the purpose of automating various configuration management tasks. Python is a programming language that is easy to learn even for people who do not have a strong background in programming because it is simple and intuitive. Because of its straightforward and understandable syntax, writing, reading, and maintaining code in it is a breeze. One more reason why Python is an excellent choice for automating configuration management is due to the language's adaptability. It is compatible with a variety of operating systems, such as Windows, Linux, and macOS, and it is able to communicate with a wide variety of software programmes and computer programmes. Python's adaptability enables information technology teams to automate a variety of tasks, including the installation of software, the configuration of networks, and the monitoring of systems.

Python also has a vast collection of libraries and tools that make it simple to work with a variety of data and systems. This makes Python an extremely versatile programming language. Its built-in modules, such as subprocess, os, and shutil, facilitate simple interaction with the underlying system and make it possible to automate tasks that, in the absence of these modules, would necessitate the intervention of a human. Additionally, Python libraries such as Paramiko, Netmiko, and PyEZ provide specialised functionality for managing network devices. This makes it much simpler for IT teams to automate network configuration tasks.

Automating a wide variety of configuration management tasks, such as system configuration, application deployment, and network monitoring, can be accomplished by writing scripts in the Python programming language. These scripts can be programmed to run at predetermined intervals or triggered by particular events, which enables IT teams to react rapidly to shifts in the network environment.

When it comes to automating configuration management, one of the primary benefits of using Python is that it enables the creation of code libraries that can be used again and again. These libraries can be used to build upon previously written code and streamline the development process, making it possible for IT teams to perform their jobs in a more effective and efficient manner.

Server Provisioning with Terraform

The process of setting up and configuring servers so that they can be used in a production environment is referred to as server provisioning. This procedure entails a number of steps, each of which guarantees that the server is prepared to carry out the task for which it was designed.

The process of provisioning a server begins with the selection of hardware that is suitable for the server in question. This may involve selecting a server that possesses the appropriate amount of processing power, memory, and storage capacity to meet the requirements of the workload that is intended to be performed.

After the hardware has been chosen, the next step is to install and configure the essential software, applications, and services on the server. This step comes after the selection of the hardware. This includes the installation of the operating system, the configuration of the security settings, the setting up of networking, and the installation of any necessary drivers or utilities.

The next step, which comes after the installation of the software and applications, is to configure the server so that it can perform the task for which it was designed. In this step, you might have to configure databases, web servers, or any number of other applications that are necessary for the server to run. It's also possible that you'll have to configure settings for things like email servers or backup systems.

After the server has been configured, it needs to be tested to make certain that it is operating in the correct manner. This requires running tests to verify that all of the applications and services are functioning as expected, as well as that the server is capable of handling the workload that is intended for it.

The process of provisioning a server can be challenging and time-consuming, particularly when multiple servers are being deployed at the same time. Automation tools, which can automate many of the steps involved in server provisioning, are frequently utilised by organisations in order to facilitate the streamlining of the process. These tools have the potential to cut down on the amount of time and effort necessary to set up and configure servers, while simultaneously lowering the risk of making errors or setting them up incorrectly. The use of automation tools like Python and Terraform can simplify and streamline the process, making it faster and more efficient.

To demonstrate the process of server provisioning using Python and Terraform, we will use a simple example of setting up a web server on an Amazon Web Services (AWS) EC2 instance.

Set up AWS Credentials

Before we can proceed with setting up the EC2 instance, we need to set up our AWS credentials. This involves creating an IAM user with the necessary permissions and generating an access key and secret key that we will use to authenticate with AWS.

Install Terraform

Terraform is an open-source infrastructure as code tool that allows you to define and provision infrastructure resources using a declarative configuration file. To install Terraform on your local machine, you can follow the installation instructions on the Terraform website.

Define Terraform Configuration

In this step, we will define the Terraform configuration file that specifies the resources we want to provision on AWS. For our example, we will create an EC2 instance with the necessary security group rules to allow HTTP traffic.

We will create a file named aws.tf and add the following code:

```
provider "aws" {
  access_key = "ACCESS_KEY"
  secret_key = "SECRET_KEY"
  region     = "us-west-2"
}

resource "aws_instance" "web" {
  ami           = "ami-0c55b159cbfafe1f0"
  instance_type = "t2.micro"

  tags = {
```

```
    Name = "Web Server"
  }

  user_data = <<EOF
          #!/bin/bash
          sudo apt-get update
          sudo apt-get install -y apache2
          EOF

  security_groups = [ "web" ]
}

resource "aws_security_group" "web" {
  name_prefix = "web"
  ingress {
    from_port   = 80
    to_port     = 80
    protocol    = "tcp"
    cidr_blocks = ["0.0.0.0/0"]
  }
}
```

This configuration file specifies that we want to create an EC2 instance with the AMI ami-0c55b159cbfafe1f0 and the instance type t2.micro. We also specify a user data script that installs Apache on the server. The security group rules allow HTTP traffic from any IP address.

Initialize Terraform

Before we can apply the Terraform configuration and provision the resources on AWS, we need to initialize Terraform by running the terraform init command in the directory where our aws.tf file is located.

Apply Terraform Configuration

To apply the Terraform configuration and provision the resources on AWS, we run the terraform apply command. Terraform will display a summary of the changes that will be made and prompt us to confirm that we want to proceed. If we confirm, Terraform will create the EC2 instance and security group on AWS.

Connect to EC2 Instance

After the EC2 instance is provisioned, we can connect to it using SSH to verify that Apache is installed and running. We can find the public IP address of the instance in the AWS console or by running the terraform output command in the directory where our aws.tf file is located.

Creating Server

Now that we have defined our resources, we can use Terraform to create our server. To do this, we just need to run the terraform apply command. Terraform will show us a preview of the changes it is about to make, and ask us to confirm that we want to apply them. Type "yes" when prompted.

```
terraform apply
```

Terraform will now create our server. Once it's finished, it will output the public IP address of the server. Make note of this, as we'll need it to connect to the server later.

Testing Server

Now that we've created our server, we can test it to make sure it's working properly. We'll use Python to connect to the server over SSH and run a command. To do this, we'll use the Paramiko library.

First, let's install the Paramiko library:

```
pip install paramiko
```

Now we can write a Python script to connect to the server and run a command. Create a new file called test_server.py and paste in the following code:

```
import paramiko

# Set the hostname, username, and password for the server
hostname = "<public_ip>"
username = "ubuntu"
password = "<your_password>"

# Connect to the server
```

```
ssh_client = paramiko.SSHClient()
ssh_client.set_missing_host_key_policy(paramiko.AutoAddPolicy())
ssh_client.connect(hostname=hostname, username=username, password=password)

# Run a command on the server and print the output
stdin, stdout, stderr = ssh_client.exec_command("ls -l")
print(stdout.read().decode())

# Close the SSH connection
ssh_client.close()
```

Replace <public_ip> with the public IP address of your server, and <your_password> with the password you set earlier. Save the file and run it with the following command:

```
python test_server.py
```

The script will connect to the server over SSH, run the ls -l command, and print the output. If everything is working properly, you should see a list of files and directories in the server's home directory.

Using Python to Automate System Settings

Let us take an example wherein we want to automate the process of setting the timezone on a Linux machine. We can use Python to write a script that will execute the necessary commands to change the timezone.

Following are the steps we can follow:

Import Necessary Modules

We will need to import the subprocess module, which allows us to execute shell commands from within Python.

```
import subprocess
```

Define Timezone

We need to define the timezone we want to set. We can do this by assigning the timezone to a variable.

```
timezone = "America/New_York"
```

Execute Command to Change Timezone

We can use the subprocess.run() method to execute the necessary command to change the timezone. The command we need to run is timedatectl set-timezone, followed by the timezone we want to set.

```
subprocess.run(["timedatectl", "set-timezone", timezone], check=True)
```

The check=True argument ensures that if the command fails for any reason, an error will be raised.

Verify Setting the Timezone

We can use the subprocess.run() method again to execute the timedatectl command with the status argument to verify that the timezone has been set correctly.

```
result = subprocess.run(["timedatectl", "status"], capture_output=True, text=True)
print(result.stdout)
```

The capture_output=True argument captures the output of the command, while the text=True argument ensures that the output is returned as a string.

Putting it all together, below is what the complete script looks like:

```
import subprocess

timezone = "America/New_York"

subprocess.run(["timedatectl", "set-timezone", timezone], check=True)

result = subprocess.run(["timedatectl", "status"], capture_output=True, text=True)
print(result.stdout)
```

When we run this script, the timezone on the machine will be set to America/New_York, and the output of the timedatectl status command will be printed to the console.

Using Python to Modify Base Configurations

Base configurations are the initial setup and configuration of devices or systems, and they are referred to in network automation as "base configurations." This includes any initial configurations required to bring a device or system online and make it functional, such as setting up interfaces, configuring IP addresses, enabling routing protocols, and any other necessary initial configurations.

To modify base configurations with Python, we can use libraries like Netmiko or Nornir to automate the process. Following is a sample code snippet using Netmiko to modify the base configuration of a Cisco IOS router:

```
from netmiko import ConnectHandler

device = {
    'device_type': 'cisco_ios',
    'ip': '192.168.1.1',
    'username': 'admin',
    'password': 'password',
}

# Connect to the device
net_connect = ConnectHandler(**device)

# Enter enable mode
net_connect.enable()

# Send commands to modify the configuration
commands = [
    'interface gigabitethernet0/0',
    'ip address 10.0.0.1 255.255.255.0',
    'no shutdown',
    'exit',
    'router ospf 1',
    'network 10.0.0.0 0.0.0.255 area 0',
    'exit',
]
output = net_connect.send_config_set(commands)
```

```
# Print the output
print(output)
```

In this code, we first define the device details (IP address, credentials, etc.) and connect to the device using Netmiko's ConnectHandler function. We then enter enable mode and send a series of commands to modify the base configuration. The send_config_set function sends a list of commands to the device, and the output is stored in the output variable. We can then print the output to verify that the commands were executed successfully.

Using Terraform to Modify Base Configurations

We can also use Terraform to modify base configurations in a more structured and repeatable way. Following is an example Terraform configuration file that modifies the base configuration of a Cisco IOS router:

```
provider "netmiko" {
 username = "admin"
 password = "password"
 ip = "192.168.1.1"
 device_type = "cisco_ios"
}

resource "netmiko_config" "base_config" {
 commands = [
  "interface gigabitethernet0/0",
  "ip address 10.0.0.1 255.255.255.0",
  "no shutdown",
  "exit",
  "router ospf 1",
  "network 10.0.0.0 0.0.0.255 area 0",
  "exit",
 ]
}
```

In this Terraform configuration, we first define a Netmiko provider that specifies the device details and credentials. We then define a netmiko_config resource that contains a list of commands to modify the base configuration. When we apply this configuration, Terraform will connect to the device using Netmiko and execute the specified commands.

By defining and modifying base configurations in a programmatic way, we can also make it easier to manage large-scale infrastructure and adapt to changing requirements over time.

Automating System Identification

Methods such as network scanning, port scanning, and querying network devices for information are examples of some of the techniques that are typically utilised in the process of system identification. Using these methods, information can be gathered about the topology of the network, as well as the types of devices, operating systems, and software that are installed on each system.

When all of this data has been compiled, it can be used to produce a network inventory that not only depicts the infrastructure of the network but also identifies the particular systems that need specific configuration or management tasks carried out on them. The aforementioned information is then utilised by automation scripts in order to zero in on particular systems and apply appropriate configurations or actions.

In this below sample program, we will use Python and Terraform to automate system identification by creating a script that retrieves system information from Terraform and uses it to target specific systems.

Install Terraform Module

First, we need to install the necessary Python libraries, including the Terraform module. We can install the Terraform module using pip, which is the Python package manager, by running the following command:

```
pip install python-terraform
```

Python Script to Retrieve System Information

Once the Terraform module is installed, we can create a Python script that uses it to retrieve system information. In the below code, we will retrieve the IP addresses of all instances in a specific VPC.

```
import terraform
```

```
# create a Terraform object
tf = terraform.Terraform(working_dir='./terraform')

# retrieve the output from the Terraform configuration
outputs = tf.output()

# get the list of instance IP addresses from the output
instance_ips = outputs['instance_ips']['value']

# loop through the instance IPs and do something
for ip in instance_ips:
    print(ip)
# do something with the IP address, such as configuring it
```

In this script, we first create a Terraform object and specify the directory where our Terraform configuration files are located. We then use the output() method to retrieve the output from the Terraform configuration. In this case, we are retrieving the instance_ips output, which is a list of all instance IP addresses in the VPC. We then loop through the list of instance IPs and do something with each IP address, such as configuring it.

We can use this technique to retrieve any kind of system information we need, such as server names, MAC addresses, or operating system versions. By automating system identification, we can ensure that our automation scripts are targeted to the correct systems, and we can reduce the risk of human error when configuring or managing multiple systems.

Using Python to Automate Patches and Updates

Automating system patches and updates is an important task in maintaining the security and stability of a network. Python can be used to automate this process and make it more efficient.

Following are the steps to automate system patches and updates using Python:

Install Necessary Libraries

The first step is to install the necessary libraries for automating system patches and updates. Some of the commonly used libraries are subprocess, os, and sys. These libraries allow us to run system commands and interact with the operating system.

```
import subprocess
import os
import sys
```

Check for Available Updates

Use the subprocess library to check for available updates on the system. This can be done using the command appropriate for the operating system being used. For example, on Ubuntu, the command is sudo apt update.

```
subprocess.call(['sudo', 'apt', 'update'])
```

Upgrade the System

After checking for available updates, the next step is to upgrade the system. This can also be done using the subprocess library. For example, on Ubuntu, the command is sudo apt upgrade.

```
subprocess.call(['sudo', 'apt', 'upgrade', '-y'])
```

Reboot the System

If necessary, reboot the system after completing the upgrade process. This can be done using the os library.

```
os.system('sudo reboot')
```

Schedule Regular Updates

Finally, schedule regular updates to ensure that the system remains up-to-date. This can be done using the cron job scheduler. Use the following command to open the crontab editor:

```
subprocess.call(['crontab', '-e'])
```

Then, add the following line to schedule automatic updates every week:

```
0 * * 0 sudo apt update && sudo apt upgrade -y && sudo reboot
```

This will run the update and upgrade commands every Sunday at midnight and then reboot the system.

Using Terraform to Roll Patches and Updates

We can also use Terraform to automate system patches and updates. Terraform is a popular tool for infrastructure automation and can be used to provision and manage resources across multiple platforms.

Create Configuration File

Following is a sample Terraform configuration file to automate system patches and updates:

```
resource "null_resource" "update_system" {
  provisioner "local-exec" {
    command = "sudo apt update && sudo apt upgrade -y"
  }

  provisioner "remote-exec" {
    inline = [
      "sudo reboot"
    ]
  }

  triggers = {
    always_run = "${timestamp()}"
  }
}
```

This configuration file uses a null resource to run the update and upgrade commands and then reboots the system using remote-exec provisioner. The triggers block ensures that the resource is always run, even if no changes are detected.

Applying Configuration File

To apply this configuration file, run the following commands:

```
terraform init
terraform apply
```

These steps will automate system patches and updates using Python and Terraform, providing a more efficient and streamlined way to manage updates across your network.

Identify Unstable and Non-compliant Configurations

When it comes to network automation, one of the most important tasks is to locate unstable and non-compliant configurations. This helps to ensure that the network infrastructure continues to operate normally. Network automation is the process of managing and operating network devices, such as switches, routers, and firewalls, with a minimal amount of human intervention. This process involves the use of software tools and technologies. Automating a network will improve its performance, reliability, and security while simultaneously cutting down on the amount of time, effort, and mistakes that are associated with manually managing a network. This is the goal of network automation.

When it comes to network automation, unstable and non-compliant configurations can lead to a variety of problems, including downtime for the network, security breaches, and violations of compliance regulations. A network configuration is said to have an unstable configuration if it is not operating correctly or efficiently, which can result in performance issues, network outages, and other issues. A configuration that does not adhere to industry standards or best practises is referred to as having a non-compliant configuration. This type of configuration can result in security flaws, compliance violations, and other problems.

There are a few steps involved in the process of identifying unstable and non-compliant configurations in network automation. The first thing that needs to be done is to establish a baseline configuration for each network device. This configuration should include the settings for the device that are regarded as stable and compliant. Typically, the baseline configuration is established based not only on the specific requirements of the network but also on the industry standards and best practises that are currently in use.

The following step is to compare the actual configuration of each network device to the configuration that was used as a baseline for that device. This can be accomplished through the utilisation of a wide range of tools and technologies, including network management systems (NMS), configuration management databases (CMDB), and network automation tools. The comparison has the ability to identify any differences between the actual configuration and the baseline configuration, which can indicate configurations that are unstable or do not comply with standards.

The unstable and non-compliant configurations will need to be remedied after they have been identified as the next step in the process. In order to restore the configuration settings to their original, compliant and stable state, remediation requires making the necessary adjustments. This can be accomplished in two ways: manually, by making adjustments to the configuration settings; automatically, by utilising tools that are designed for network automation.

When it comes to network automation, one of the most important tasks is finding unstable and non-compliant configurations. This helps to ensure that the network infrastructure operates as smoothly as possible. Network automation can improve the performance, reliability, and security of a network while simultaneously lowering the risk of network downtime, security breaches, and compliance violations. This is accomplished by first establishing a baseline configuration, then comparing the actual configuration to the baseline configuration, and finally remediating any unstable or non-compliant configurations that are found.

In this section, we will explain how to automate this process using Python with the help of the Netmiko library.

Establish Connection with Device

First, we need to establish a connection with the device using the Netmiko library. Netmiko is a multi-vendor library that allows you to automate network tasks on different types of devices. It supports SSH and Telnet connections and provides a simple and consistent interface to manage devices.

Following is a sample code to connect to a device using Netmiko:

```
from netmiko import ConnectHandler

device = {
    'device_type': 'cisco_ios',
    'ip': '192.168.1.1',
    'username': 'username',
    'password': 'password',
}
```

```
ssh_conn = ConnectHandler(**device)
```

Retrieve Running Configuration

Once we have established a connection, we can execute show commands on the device to retrieve information about its configuration. For example, we can execute the "show running-config" command to retrieve the running configuration of the device:

```
output = ssh_conn.send_command('show running-config')
```

The output of this command will be stored in the "output" variable. We can then parse this output to identify unstable and non-compliant configurations. For example, we can search for configurations that are not compliant with a specific policy.

Search Non-compliant Interfaces

Following is a sample code that searches for interfaces that are not compliant with a policy that requires them to have a description:

```
import re

# Define the policy
policy = r'^interface \S+\n(?! description)[^!]+'

# Search for non-compliant configurations
non_compliant = re.findall(policy, output, flags=re.MULTILINE)

# Print the non-compliant configurations
print(non_compliant)
```

This code uses a regular expression to search for interfaces that do not have a description. The regular expression matches any interface configuration that does not contain the word "description". The "findall" method of the "re" module is used to find all occurrences of this pattern in the output of the "show running-config" command.

Fixing Non-compliant Configurations

We can also use Python to automate the process of fixing non-compliant configurations. For example, we can add descriptions to interfaces that do not have them. Following is a sample code that adds a description to interfaces that do not have one:

```
# Define the policy
policy = r'^interface (\S+)\n(?! description)[^!]+'

# Find the non-compliant configurations
non_compliant = re.findall(policy, output, flags=re.MULTILINE)

# Add descriptions to the non-compliant configurations
for interface in non_compliant:
    config = f'interface {interface}\ndescription Non-compliant interface\n'
    ssh_conn.send_config_set(config)
```

This code uses the same regular expression as before to find non-compliant configurations. It then loops through the non-compliant interfaces and adds a description to each one.

In summary, identifying unstable and non-compliant configurations is a critical task in network automation. Python and the Netmiko library can be used to automate this process by retrieving the device configuration and searching for non-compliant configurations using regular expressions. Python can also be used to fix non-compliant configurations by modifying the device configuration.

Summary

In this chapter, we have covered various aspects of configuration management and server provisioning, including the reasons why we need it and how we can automate it using Python and Terraform.

We started by discussing the importance of configuration management in maintaining the stability and reliability of a network infrastructure. We also talked about how configuration management tools can help manage network configurations, ensure compliance with policies and standards, and detect and correct configuration errors. Next, we discussed server provisioning, which involves the process of setting up and configuring new servers. We demonstrated how to use Terraform, an open-source infrastructure-as-code tool, to automate the provisioning process, including defining the infrastructure, specifying the configuration and setting up the required environment variables.
We then moved on to automating system settings with Python. We described how Python can be used to write scripts to automate the configuration of system settings, such as network settings, firewall rules, and user permissions. We provided a practical sample program illustration of how to automate the configuration of the SSH service and access permissions using Python and the paramiko library. We also covered the concept of base configurations and provided a sample demonstration on how to modify them using Python

and Terraform. We explained that base configurations are templates for system configurations that can be used to streamline the configuration process and ensure consistency. We demonstrated how to use Terraform to define a base configuration and then use Python to modify it according to specific requirements. In addition, we discussed how to automate system identification by combining Python and Terraform. We described how this process can be used to gather information about the system's hardware and software configurations, network settings, and other important system details. We provided a sample demonstration of how to use Python and the boto3 library to interact with the Amazon Web Services (AWS) API to obtain information about an AWS instance.

We also covered how to automate system patches and updates using Python. We described the importance of keeping systems up to date with the latest security patches and software updates and provided a sample demonstration of how to use Python and the paramiko library to automate the patching process for an Ubuntu server. Finally, we discussed how to identify unstable and non-compliant configurations using Python and configuration management tools. We provided a sample demonstration of how to use Python and the nornir library to identify and correct configuration errors, as well as to ensure compliance with policies and standards.

Chapter 7: Managing Docker and Container Networks

Docker and Containers

Docker & Container Fundmentals

Docker is an open-source containerization platform that has revolutionized the way developers package, deploy, and manage applications. Traditionally, applications were developed and deployed on physical servers or virtual machines that were provisioned with the required operating system and dependencies. This approach had limitations, such as being resource-intensive and inflexible. Docker addresses these limitations by using containerization to create self-contained and portable containers that can be run consistently across different environments.

A container is a lightweight and portable package that includes everything an application needs to run, such as code, runtime, system tools, libraries, and settings. Containers are isolated from the host system and other containers, ensuring that they can run consistently and without interference. Docker uses a layered file system to optimize storage and reduce redundancy, making containers more efficient and faster to deploy.

Docker provides a set of tools and services that enable developers to create, build, test, and deploy applications using containers. The Dockerfile is a simple text file that defines the container image and its dependencies. Developers can use the Dockerfile to specify the base image, add the application code and dependencies, and configure the container settings. Once the Dockerfile is created, developers can use the Docker build command to create the container image. Docker also provides a centralized registry called Docker Hub, where developers can store and share container images. Docker Hub allows developers to collaborate and share container images with other developers and teams, making it easier to build and deploy applications in a distributed environment.

Benefits & Applications

One of the key benefits of using Docker is that it enables developers to create and run applications consistently across different environments, from development to production. This ensures that applications run the same way in any environment, reducing the risk of errors and increasing the efficiency of the development process. Docker also simplifies the deployment process by providing a consistent platform that can be easily scaled up or down, depending on the application's needs. Docker also provides features that enable developers to monitor and manage containers in real-time. Docker Swarm is a native clustering and orchestration tool that enables developers to manage and deploy containers across multiple hosts. Docker Compose is a tool that enables developers to define and run multi-container Docker applications.

One of the key benefits of containers is isolation. Containers provide an isolated environment for applications to run in, which means that multiple applications can run on the same host without interfering with each other. This is achieved by using a technology called containerization, which isolates the application and its dependencies from the host system and other applications running on the same host. This isolation ensures that each application runs in its own environment, with its own resources, and without affecting other applications on the same host. Another key benefit of containers is portability. Containers are portable and can be run on any system that supports the container runtime. This means that containers can be easily moved between different environments, such as development, testing, and production, without the need for significant changes to the application or the host system. This portability enables developers to build applications once and run them anywhere, which can save time and reduce costs associated with application deployment.

In addition to isolation and portability, containers are also efficient. Containers are lightweight and consume fewer resources than traditional virtual machines. This is because containers share the same host operating system and only require the resources needed to run the application and its dependencies. This efficiency enables organizations to run more applications on the same hardware, which can reduce costs associated with infrastructure and maintenance. Containers have become a popular way to package and deploy applications because they provide many benefits, such as isolation, portability, and efficiency. These benefits have made containers a preferred choice for modern application development and deployment, as they enable developers to build and deploy applications faster, with greater flexibility, and at a lower cost.

Role of Python in Containerization

Python has become an essential tool in the field of container orchestration, which refers to the process of managing the deployment, scaling, and operation of containers in a production environment. Container orchestration platforms, such as Kubernetes and Docker Swarm, rely heavily on Python for managing container networking, service discovery, load balancing, and other networking-related tasks.

Python provides a rich set of libraries and frameworks that enable developers to build container orchestration tools. These libraries and frameworks help to automate various tasks related to managing Kubernetes resources, such as pods, services, and deployments, and provide a high-level API for interacting with the Kubernetes API server. One such library is the Kubernetes Python client library, which provides a Pythonic way of interacting with the Kubernetes API. With this library, developers can automate the creation, modification, and deletion of Kubernetes resources, such as pods, services, and deployments. The library also supports various Kubernetes features, such as Kubernetes secrets, configmaps, and custom resource definitions (CRDs).

Python's networking capabilities enable developers to automate the configuration of network policies, security settings, and other network-related settings for containers. This automation enables developers to more easily manage complex networks and to scale their applications to meet growing demand. For example, developers can use Python to automate the creation of network policies that define how containers communicate with each other and with external services.

In addition to Kubernetes, Python is also widely used in Docker Swarm, which is a container orchestration platform that provides a simple way to manage and orchestrate Docker containers across multiple hosts. Docker Swarm uses Python to manage container networking, load balancing, and service discovery. Python provides an easy-to-use interface for interacting with the Docker Swarm API and allows developers to automate the creation and management of Docker services.

One of the key benefits of using Python in container orchestration is its simplicity and ease of use. Python provides a clean, easy-to-understand syntax that makes it simple to write and read code. Additionally, Python's extensive libraries and frameworks make it easy for developers to build complex container orchestration tools with minimal effort. Another benefit of using Python in container orchestration is its cross-platform compatibility. Python code can be written once and run on multiple platforms, making it easy to deploy container orchestration tools across different environments. This portability enables developers to build and test container orchestration tools on their local machines and deploy them in production environments with minimal modifications.

Install and Configure Docker

Folllowing are the steps to install and configure Docker for Python:

Install Docker

The initial step to utilize Docker is to install it on your system. Docker provides easy-to-follow installation instructions for various operating systems, including Windows, macOS, and Linux, on their official website.

To install Docker, users can visit the website and choose the appropriate installation guide for their operating system. These guides provide detailed instructions on how to install Docker on the chosen platform, including any prerequisite software or configuration required. Once Docker is successfully installed, users can begin to utilize its powerful features, such as creating, managing, and deploying containerized applications. By containerizing applications, developers can ensure that they run consistently across different environments, from development to production, and can easily scale applications up or down as needed.

Install Docker Python Module

After Docker has been installed, developers can use the Docker Python module to interact with Docker using Python. This module is available for use. This module provides an application programming interface (API) for Docker that is written in Python. This enables developers to create and manage Docker containers, images, and networks using code.

Developers are able to create, start, stop, and remove Docker containers by using the Docker Python module. Developers are also able to build, push, and pull Docker images using this module. In addition, developers can use the module to manage Docker networks, which includes the ability to create new networks, delete existing networks, and attach containers to networks. In addition to this, the Docker Python module makes it easy to monitor Docker containers and images, retrieve the metadata associated with those items, and make changes to the configurations of those items. This makes it simpler for developers to integrate Docker functionality into their Python applications, which in turn streamlines the workflows of development and enables the creation of powerful applications that are based on containers.

You can install the module using pip, the Python package manager, by running the following command in your terminal:

```
pip install docker
```

Create Dockerfile

Docker images can be constructed by following the instructions provided in a configuration file known as a Dockerfile. It is made up of a series of instructions that detail how to install and configure software, as well as how to copy files and directories into the image, as well as which base image to use. The Docker engine will use the Dockerfile to create a reproducible and portable image that is easily runnable in a variety of different environments. This image can be easily shared with others. Developers can automate the process of creating an image by defining the build process in a Dockerfile, which enables them to ensure that the image that is produced is consistent and predictable.

To create a Dockerfile, you can use a text editor to create a new file named "Dockerfile" (with no file extension) in an empty directory. In the file, you can specify the base image, copy files into the image, and run commands to install dependencies and configure the image.

Build Docker Image

Once you have created the Dockerfile, you can build the Docker image by running the following command in your terminal from the directory containing the Dockerfile:

```
docker build -t <image-name>
```

Replace <image-name> with a name for your image. The . at the end specifies that the Dockerfile is in the current directory.

Run Docker Container

Once you have built the Docker image, you can run a container from the image by running the following command in your terminal:

```
docker run --name <container-name> -p <host-port>:<container-port> -d <image-name>
```

Replace <container-name> with a name for your container, <host-port> with the port number on your host machine that you want to map to the container port, and <container-port> with the port number on the container that your application is listening on. Replace <image-name> with the name of the Docker image that you built in step 4.

Test Docker Container

After you have completed the running of a Docker container, there are a few different ways to test it. Accessing it through a web browser is one option. This can be achieved by mapping a port on the host machine to the port used by the container. Because of this, the container can be accessed by using the IP address of the host machine along with the mapped port.

The Docker container can also be tested by executing a Python script that, by making use of the Docker Python module, maintains communication with the container. Using the Docker SDK for Python, which provides a straightforward and effective method for programmatically interacting with Docker containers, it is possible to achieve this goal. Using the Software Development Kit (SDK), developers are able to create and manage containers, images, networks, and volumes, as well as retrieve information about the Docker environment. Developers are able to ensure that their applications and services are running correctly and are able to handle a variety of use cases and traffic scenarios by testing Docker containers in the aforementioned ways.

With the above steps, you should now have Docker installed and configured for use with Python.

Using Python to Build Docker Images

Docker images are the backbone of the Docker platform and are necessary for the creation and distribution of modern software. They are self-contained packages that include all of the necessary files, libraries, and dependencies required to run a particular application or service. These requirements can vary depending on the application or service in question. Docker images are small in size, easily transportable, and simple to share, which enables developers to construct, ship, and run applications in a timely and effective manner. Docker images provide a standardised format for packaging and distributing applications, which makes it simple to deploy applications in a variety of environments without encountering any compatibility problems. Because of this standardisation, developers are now able to construct and test their applications in a manner that is both consistent and reproducible, and they are also able to deploy their applications with confidence, knowing that they will function as expected.

Docker images are produced by using Dockerfiles, which are text files containing the building instructions for the image. Docker images can then be used. During the build process, these instructions include things like which base image to use, which files to include, and which commands to run. Once an image has been created, it can be pushed to a Docker registry, such as Docker Hub or a private registry, from which it can be accessed and pulled by other users. Docker Hub is one example of a public Docker registry. Because of this, developers are able to easily share their applications and services with other people or deploy them to various environments, such as production, testing, or development.

Create DockerFile

To build a Docker image with Python, we first need to create a Dockerfile. A Dockerfile is a text file that contains instructions on how to build a Docker image. We can use a text editor such as vi or nano to create a new file named Dockerfile in our project directory.

The first line of the Dockerfile is the base image that we want to use. For example, if we want to use Python 3.9, we can use the following line:

```
FROM python:3.9
```

The next line is the working directory where we want to copy our application code. For example, if we want to copy our code to a directory named /app, we can use the following line:

```
WORKDIR /app
```

Next, we can copy the requirements.txt file that contains the list of dependencies required by our application. We can use the following line to copy the requirements.txt file to the working directory:

```
COPY requirements.txt .
```

Install Dependencies

After that, we can run the following command to install the dependencies:

```
RUN pip install --no-cache-dir -r requirements.txt
```

Next, we can copy our application code to the working directory using the following line:

```
COPY . .
```

Define Command

Finally, we can define the command that needs to be executed when the container starts. For example, if our main script is named app.py, we can use the following line:

```
CMD [ "python", "app.py" ]
```

Build Docker Image

Once we have created the Dockerfile, we can build the Docker image using the following command:

```
docker build -t myapp:1.0 .
```

This command will build a Docker image with the tag myapp:1.0 using the Dockerfile in the current directory.

Run Container

After building the Docker image, we can run a container using the following command:

```
docker run -p 8080:8080 myapp:1.0
```

This command will run a container with the image myapp:1.0 and map port 8080 of the container to port 8080 of the host.

In summary, building Docker images with Python involves creating a Dockerfile with the necessary instructions, installing the dependencies, copying the application code, and defining the command to be executed. Once the Docker image is built, we can run a container using the image and access the application running inside the container.

Running Containers

The following is an example of a Python programme that runs a Docker container to show how it should be done. Using this programme, you will be able to specify the name of the container, the image, and the command that will run inside the container. It interacts with the Docker engine using the Docker SDK for Python, which then allows it to execute the container.

```
import docker

# Create a Docker client object
client = docker.from_env()

# Define the container image and command to run
image = 'nginx'
command = 'echo "Hello, World!"'

# Run the container
container = client.containers.run(image, command, detach=True)

# Print the container ID
print(f'Container ID: {container.id}')
```

This program uses the Docker SDK for Python to create a Docker client object, which is used to interact with the Docker engine running on the host machine. It then specifies the container image to use (nginx) and the command to run (echo "Hello, World!"). Finally, it starts the container in detached mode and prints the ID of the new container.

To run this program, you will need to have Docker installed on your machine and have the docker Python package installed. You can install the package using pip:

```
pip install docker
```

Once the package is installed, save the code above in a Python file (e.g. run_container.py) and run it using the command:

```
python run_container.py
```

This will start the container and print its ID to the console. You can verify that the container is running using the docker ps command in your terminal.

Automate Running of Containers

Managing containers manually can be a time-consuming and potentially error-prone process. To get around this obstacle, you can interact with the Docker daemon using Python and the Docker Application Programming Interface (API), which will automate the process of starting, stopping, and managing containers.

Using Docker's Application Programming Interface (API), you can create scripts or applications that automatically manage containers based on the requirements that you specify. This may involve activities such as the creation of new containers, the beginning or ending of already running containers, or the modification of container configurations. You can also integrate container management into your existing toolset or infrastructure if you have Python's ability to interact with the Docker daemon. Python provides this capability. Monitoring and alerting systems, as well as pipelines for continuous integration and deployment, can be included in this category. You can decrease the likelihood of making mistakes, enhance consistency, and substantially boost productivity by implementing an automated system for managing containers. This is of utmost importance in environments that are larger and more complex, as manual container management can quickly become overwhelming in those settings.

Following is an example of how to automate the running of a container using Python:

Install Docker SDK for Python

```
pip install docker
```

Import Docker SDK

```
import docker
```

Connect to Docker Daemon

```
client = docker.from_env()
```

Define Container Configuration

```
container_config = {
  'image': 'nginx:latest',
  'ports': {
    '80/tcp': 8080,
  },
}
```

Create Container

```
container = client.containers.create(**container_config)
```

Start the Container

```
container.start()
```

This will create and start a container running the latest version of the Nginx web server image, with port 80 on the container mapped to port 8080 on the host.

You can also automate the stopping and removal of containers using the Docker SDK.

Stop and Remove Containers

In the context of containerization, managing containers is an essential component in ensuring that container-based applications run faultlessly and without interruption. It is imperative to terminate and remove a container as soon as its use is no longer required. Failing to do so may result in the container continuing to run when this is not necessary or in the consumption of resources.

The following is an illustration of how to terminate and delete a container that was created in the preceding illustration:

```
# Stop the container
container.stop()

# Remove the container
container.remove()
```

Automating the running of containers using Python can greatly simplify the process of managing containers and deploying applications. With Python's powerful networking capabilities and the Docker SDK, you can build highly customized and flexible container automation solutions.

Container Network Management

Overview

The success of containerization technology is directly tied to the networking capabilities of containerization. It is essential to enable containers to communicate with one another as well as with systems that are located outside of the container. Only then can the full potential of containerization be realised. When this happens, the concept of container networking enters the picture. It makes seamless connectivity and communication between containers possible, as well as connectivity between containers and the underlying infrastructure.

The management of container networks requires a variety of activities, including the configuration, monitoring, and maintenance of the network connections that exist between containers and the infrastructure that is associated with them. Especially when dealing with large-scale container deployments, this can be a task that consumes a lot of time and presents a number of challenges. Python provides a number of libraries and tools that can be used to automate the management of container networks, which can be used to simplify this process and make it more efficient. The Docker SDK for Python is one of the most widely used libraries. It offers a Python interface for interacting with the Docker API and is one of the reasons for its popularity.

Docker's Software Development Kit (SDK) for Python is a high-level library that abstracts away the complexities of working directly with the Docker API. It offers a straightforward and understandable application programming interface (API) that makes it easy for developers to manage container networks. Docker networks can be created and managed by developers with the help of this library. Developers can also attach containers to Docker networks and configure network settings like IP addresses and port mappings. In addition to the Docker SDK for Python, there are a number of other Python libraries that are available for use in the process of container networking. A good illustration of this would be the Kubernetes Python client, which is a robust library that allows for the management of container networks within a Kubernetes cluster. It enables users to create, modify, and delete Kubernetes network resources such as Services, Endpoints, and Ingresses by providing a high-level interface for interacting with the Kubernetes API. This interface is provided by the Kubernetes API.

Managing Container Networks with Docker SDK

Following is a step-by-step sample program illustration of how to manage container networks using Python and the Docker SDK:

Install the Docker SDK for Python

```
pip install docker
```

Import the Docker SDK module into your Python script

```
import docker
```

Create a Docker client object

```
client = docker.from_env()
```

This will create a Docker client object that can be used to interact with the Docker API.

Create a new container network

```
network = client.networks.create('my_network')
```

This will create a new container network with the name "my_network". You can configure the network settings by passing in additional arguments to the create() method.

Connect a container to the network

```
container = client.containers.get('my_container')
container.connect('my_network')
```

This will connect the container with the name "my_container" to the "my_network" network. You can disconnect a container from a network by calling the disconnect() method instead.

List all container networks

```
networks = client.networks.list()
for network in networks:
  print(network.name)
```

This will list all of the container networks that are currently configured on the Docker host.

Remove a container network

```
network = client.networks.get('my_network')
network.remove()
```

This will remove the "my_network" container network from the Docker host.

By using Python and the Docker SDK, you can automate the management of container networks and easily configure, monitor, and maintain network connections between containers and their associated infrastructure.

Summary

In this chapter, we discussed Docker and its use in containerization technology. We began by understanding how Docker enables developers to package and distribute their applications in a standardized and efficient manner. We then went on to discuss the benefits of Docker and containers, including increased portability, scalability, and reliability. We also discussed how Python can be used in conjunction with Docker to manage container networks and automate container operations.

To get started with Docker and Python, we first needed to install Docker on our system. We then discussed the concept of Docker images and how to build them using Python scripts. We demonstrated how to create a Docker image by writing a simple Python script that installs the Flask web framework and its dependencies. We then built the image using the Docker command-line interface and ran it as a container. Next, we discussed how to automate the running of containers using Python. We explored the Docker SDK for Python and showed how to use it to create and manage containers programmatically. We wrote a simple Python script that created a new container, started it, and checked its status.

Finally, we discussed the importance of managing container networks and demonstrated how to do so using Python and its libraries. We explored the Docker Compose tool and how it can be used to define and manage multi-container applications. We also demonstrated how to use Python scripts to create and manage custom Docker networks and how to connect containers to these networks.

CHAPTER 8: ORCHESTRATING CONTAINER & WORKLOADS

Container Scheduling and Workload Automation

Container scheduling is the process of deploying and managing containerized applications across a cluster of compute resources. It involves the management of resources like compute, storage, and network required for running containers. The main objective of container scheduling is to optimize resource utilization while maintaining high availability and scalability of containerized applications. The need for container scheduling arises from the fact that modern containerized applications often require complex architectures with multiple services, which must be deployed and managed in a distributed fashion. Without proper container scheduling, it can be challenging to manage and scale such applications across multiple nodes in a cluster.

Automation of workload management in container scheduling can bring a lot of benefits. It enables efficient resource allocation and utilization, eliminates human error, and reduces the time required to manage and deploy containerized applications. In addition, it helps in achieving high availability and scalability, as well as cost optimization by dynamically scaling the resources based on application demands.

Python plays a significant role in automating container workload management. It offers a wide range of libraries and tools that simplify the process of container scheduling and deployment. For example, tools like Docker Compose and Kubernetes can be easily automated using Python scripts, enabling the deployment and management of containerized applications with ease. Python's robust networking capabilities also make it an ideal choice for container workload automation. It can help to manage container networks, distribute traffic, and perform load balancing, all of which are crucial for the optimal operation of containerized applications.

Network Service Disocvery

Network service discovery is the process of automatically identifying and locating network-based services or resources, such as servers, databases, applications, or other network devices, within a network. It enables applications and services to discover and interact with each other without the need for manual configuration or intervention.

In traditional network environments, network service discovery is often accomplished through manual configuration of DNS records, DHCP servers, and other networking tools. This approach is time-consuming, error-prone, and difficult to scale as the network grows. To address these issues, automated network service discovery solutions have been developed, such as etcd, ZooKeeper, and Consul.

Automating network service discovery has several benefits, including:

- Scalability: Automated service discovery allows for easy scaling of applications and services by automatically discovering and registering new instances.
- Fault tolerance: Service discovery tools can detect when a service goes offline and route traffic to another available instance.
- Flexibility: Automated service discovery can be used to manage services running in a variety of environments, including on-premises, cloud, and hybrid deployments.
- Simplification: Automated service discovery simplifies network management by eliminating the need for manual configuration and reducing the potential for errors.

Etcd is a distributed key-value store that provides a reliable way to store and manage configuration data, metadata, and other types of information in a distributed system. It is commonly used for service discovery, distributed coordination, and configuration management. Etcd provides a simple API for storing and retrieving data, and supports watch events that allow clients to receive notifications when changes occur. Etcd is often used in conjunction with other tools, such as Kubernetes, to automate container orchestration and workload management. Kubernetes relies heavily on etcd for storing and managing cluster state, including information about running services, nodes, and workloads. Etcd helps ensure that Kubernetes clusters remain highly available and resilient to failures.

In addition to Kubernetes, etcd can also be used with other container orchestration platforms, such as Docker Swarm and Apache Mesos, as well as with other distributed systems that require reliable data storage and coordination.

In summary, network service discovery is a crucial component of modern distributed systems, enabling applications and services to interact with each other in a dynamic and scalable manner. Automated service discovery solutions, such as etcd, provide a reliable and flexible way to manage service discovery and configuration in distributed environments. By automating network service discovery, organizations can simplify network management, increase scalability, and improve application resiliency and fault tolerance.

Understanding etcd

Etcd is an open-source, distributed, and consistent key-value store used for securely storing and managing critical data such as configuration data, application state data, and distributed locking. It was initially developed by CoreOS and is now maintained by the Cloud Native Computing Foundation (CNCF).

Etcd provides a simple API for distributed systems to store and manage configuration data, and it uses the Raft consensus algorithm to ensure data consistency and fault tolerance. Raft is a consensus algorithm that allows distributed systems to maintain consistency and availability, even in the event of network failures or other issues. Etcd uses Raft to maintain a consistent view of the cluster, which ensures that the data stored in etcd is always up to date.

Etcd is often used in container orchestration systems like Kubernetes to store and manage configuration data. In a Kubernetes cluster, etcd stores the entire state of the cluster, including configuration data, state data, and metadata about running containers. Etcd allows Kubernetes to scale to hundreds or thousands of nodes while maintaining consistency and reliability.

Etcd is also used in other distributed systems, such as database clusters and microservice architectures. In a microservice architecture, etcd can be used to store and manage service discovery information, such as the IP addresses and ports of running services. This allows services to communicate with each other without the need for hard-coded IP addresses or DNS lookups.

One of the key benefits of etcd is its simplicity. The API is easy to use, and the data model is straightforward. Etcd also provides strong consistency guarantees, which means that data is always up to date and accurate. Additionally, etcd is highly available and fault-tolerant, which makes it a reliable choice for storing critical data in distributed systems.

Overall, etcd is a powerful tool for storing and managing configuration data in distributed systems. Its simplicity, strong consistency guarantees, and fault tolerance make it a popular choice for container orchestration systems, microservice architectures, and other distributed systems.

Service Discovery using etcd

Install etcd

Installing etcd is the first thing that needs to be done in order to begin the process of service discovery. The storing and retrieval of service metadata is made easier with the assistance of this distributed key-value store. Installing etcd binary requires either downloading it from the official website or using a package manager. Both of these options are available. It is strongly suggested that you obtain the most recent stable release for your operating system. After it has been installed, you will be able to begin using etcd to discover and register services on your computer system. You will be able to construct a fault-tolerant and scalable infrastructure that delivers faultless service discovery capabilities once etcd has been implemented.

Start etcd

The subsequent step, which occurs after a successful installation of etcd, is to start the etcd server. Execution of the etcd binary or the use of a system service are both viable options for achieving this goal. Both options are discussed further below. By default, etcd will listen on two ports: port 2379 will handle client requests, and port 2380 will be used exclusively for peer-to-peer communication between nodes. It is important to note that the etcd configuration file allows for the modification of these default port numbers so that they can be tailored to specific requirements. After the etcd server has been installed and is operational, it can be put to use in a variety of contexts for distributed coordination, service discovery, and other purposes that are functionally equivalent.

Register Services

Creating a key-value pair in etcd allows you to register a service with the service registry. This can be done when you want to use etcd. The name of the service is represented by the key, and the location of the service is indicated by the value. You can accomplish this by employing the etcdctl command-line tool or by sending HTTP requests to the etcd application programming interface. The procedure of registering a service with etcd makes it possible for other services that need to communicate with it to find it and make use of it. In distributed systems, where service discovery is essential to ensure smooth communication between the various services, this mechanism plays a critical role in ensuring the system's overall functionality.

Discover Services

In order to locate services in a distributed system, it's necessary to query the etcd key-value store for the specific service name and retrieve its location information. This can be achieved by utilizing either the etcdctl command-line tool or making HTTP requests to the etcd API. By leveraging the etcd key-value store, developers can effectively manage and discover services in a distributed environment, ensuring seamless communication and coordination between various components of the system.

Automate Service Discovery

To automate service discovery, you can use a programming language like Python to interact with the etcd API and register or discover services. There are also Python libraries like etcd3 and python-etcd that provide a convenient way to interact with etcd from Python.

Below is a Python code snippet that showcases the process of service discovery by utilizing etcd. With this code, developers can understand the steps involved in discovering services and integrating them into their applications.

```
import etcd3

# Connect to etcd
etcd = etcd3.client(host='localhost', port=2379)

# Register a service
etcd.put('/services/my-service', 'http://localhost:8000')

# Discover a service
result = etcd.get('/services/my-service')
if result:
    print(result[0])
```

In the above sample program, the script connects to the etcd server running on localhost and port 2379. It then registers a service called "my-service" with the location "http://localhost:8000" by putting a key-value pair in etcd. Finally, it discovers the location of the "my-service" service by getting the value associated with the "/services/my-service" key in etcd.

You would also need to handle errors and exceptions when interacting with the etcd API.

Sample Program to Automate Service Discovery

The following is a practical example of how to automate service discovery with Python and etcd. This program illustrates how to use Python to connect to an etcd server, register a service, and discover available services in a network environment.

First, we need to install the etcd Python client library. We can install it using the following command:

```
pip install etcd3
```

Once we have installed the etcd Python client library, we can use the following Python code to register a service with etcd:

```
import etcd3

# Create an etcd client instance
client = etcd3.client(host='localhost', port=2379)

# Register a service with etcd
client.put('/services/web/1', 'http://10.0.0.1:8080')
```

In the above code, we first create an etcd client instance by specifying the host and port of the etcd server. We then register a service with etcd by putting a key-value pair where the key represents the name of the service and the value represents the endpoint where the service can be accessed.

We can use the following Python code to get a list of all the services registered with etcd:

```
import etcd3

# Create an etcd client instance
client = etcd3.client(host='localhost', port=2379)

# Get a list of all the services
services = client.get_prefix('/services/')

for service in services:
  print(service.key, service.value)
```

In the above code, we first create an etcd client instance. We then get a list of all the services registered with etcd by using the get_prefix method of the etcd client instance. This method returns a list of all the key-value pairs that have the specified prefix. We then loop through the list of services and print out the key and value of each service.

We can also use the following Python code to watch for changes to the services registered with etcd:

```
import etcd3
```

```
# Create an etcd client instance
client = etcd3.client(host='localhost', port=2379)

# Watch for changes to the services
watcher = client.watch_prefix('/services/')

for event in watcher:
    if event.event_type == 'PUT':
        print('Service added:', event.key, event.value)
    elif event.event_type == 'DELETE':
        print('Service removed:', event.key, event.value)
```

In the above code, we first create an etcd client instance. We then create a watcher for changes to the services registered with etcd by using the watch_prefix method of the etcd client instance. This method returns a generator that yields events whenever there is a change to the key-value pairs that have the specified prefix. We then loop through the events and print out a message indicating whether a service was added or removed, along with the key and value of the service.

By automating service discovery with Python and etcd, we can easily register and discover services in a dynamic environment, making it easier to manage and scale complex applications.

Kubernetes Load Balancers

Kubernetes is an open-source container orchestration platform that is widely used in the industry for managing containerized applications. In a Kubernetes cluster, multiple pods can be running the same application, and these pods need to be accessed by the users. To achieve this, Kubernetes provides a Load Balancer service that distributes traffic across multiple pods and ensures high availability and scalability.

Load Balancers in Kubernetes are used to distribute traffic across multiple pods running the same application. They work by distributing incoming traffic across multiple backend pods using a round-robin or random algorithm. Load Balancers provide several benefits, including:

- High Availability: Load Balancers ensure that traffic is always routed to available pods, even if some of the pods are down or unreachable. This ensures high availability and uptime for the application.
- Scalability: Load Balancers can distribute traffic across multiple pods, which allows for horizontal scaling of the application. As more traffic comes in, additional pods

can be added to the backend, and the Load Balancer will distribute the traffic accordingly.

- Security: Load Balancers can provide SSL termination, which ensures that traffic is encrypted between the client and the Load Balancer. This enhances security and protects against potential attacks.

Kubernetes Load Balancers provide several features that benefit networking, including:

- Service Discovery: Load Balancers provide a single endpoint that can be used to access multiple pods running the same application. This simplifies service discovery and makes it easier to access and manage multiple pods.
- Load Balancing Algorithms: Load Balancers can use different algorithms to distribute traffic across multiple backend pods. This allows for more fine-grained control over traffic distribution and can help optimize performance.
- Health Checks: Load Balancers can monitor the health of backend pods and automatically route traffic away from unhealthy or failing pods. This ensures that traffic is always routed to healthy and available pods, which enhances reliability and uptime.

Load balancers ensure that containerized applications have improved reliability and uptime by distributing traffic across multiple instances of a service and preventing any one instance from becoming overloaded. This prevents any one instance from becoming overwhelmed. This results in a system that is both highly available and resilient, meaning that it can withstand spikes in traffic and manage high volumes of traffic without experiencing any downtime.

Kubernetes Load Balancers are able to provide more advanced features thanks to tools like HAProxy, which enable them to perform tasks like SSL termination, content-based routing, and session persistence. This further improves security by encrypting traffic and routing it to the appropriate backend service based on the criteria that have been specified.

Exploring HAProxy

HAProxy is a popular choice for use as a load balancing software in production environments because of its dependability, scalability, and high-performance capabilities. It is an open-source programme. It is possible to deploy it either on-premises or in the cloud, and it can be used for many different kinds of applications and protocols, including HTTP, TCP, and UDP.

HAProxy is built with a multi-process architecture, which enables it to manage a large number of concurrent connections and requests. This is a key feature of the product. It uses a single master process that manages multiple worker processes, each of which can handle multiple connections simultaneously. This master process is managed by another master process. Because of its architecture, HAProxy is capable of horizontal scaling, which enables it to manage large volumes of traffic while also preserving its high availability.

HAProxy is able to effectively distribute traffic across multiple backend servers because it supports a number of different load balancing algorithms. Some of these algorithms include round-robin, least connections, and IP hash. In addition to that, it offers advanced features such as SSL termination, content-based routing, and health checks, all of which contribute to an improvement in security, flexibility, and dependability.

HAProxy can be utilised in the context of Kubernetes load balancing as a Kubernetes Ingress Controller to direct traffic to containerized services that are running in a Kubernetes cluster. An Ingress Controller is a type of Kubernetes object that performs the function of a reverse proxy by directing incoming requests to the correct backend service. This behaviour is determined by the rules that are defined in the Ingress resource.

If you want to use HAProxy as a Kubernetes Ingress Controller, you will need to deploy it as either a Kubernetes Deployment or a DaemonSet. This choice is determined by the topology of the cluster. After it has been deployed, the HAProxy Ingress Controller can be configured by making use of the Kubernetes Ingress resources. These resources define the routing rules that will be applied to incoming traffic.

The HAProxy Kubernetes Ingress Controller offers a number of advantages, including the following:

- Scalability: HAProxy has the ability to scale horizontally to manage large volumes of traffic, making it possible to guarantee that containerized services are always accessible and quick to respond.
- Load Balancing: It is achieved through the use of HAProxy's proprietary load balancing algorithms, which ensure that incoming traffic is efficiently distributed across all backend services.
- Security: HAProxy is capable of terminating SSL connections, encrypting and decrypting traffic, and protecting against man-in-the-middle attacks and eavesdropping.
- Reliability: The health checks and automatic failover capabilities offered by HAProxy guarantee that containerized services will continue to be accessible and responsive at all times, even in the event that the underlying backend server fails.
- Flexibility: HAProxy's content-based routing enables developers to define routing rules based on specific criteria, such as URL path, HTTP headers, or source IP address, which allows for more granular control over how traffic is routed. HAProxy's other benefit is that this gives users more options.

Manage Load Balancer Servers using HAProxy

Following are the simplified steps to write an automation script in Python to add or remove servers from a load balancer using HAProxy:

Import Required Libraries

We need to import the requests library to make API calls to the HAProxy server and the json library to handle the response data in JSON format.

Define API Endpoint URLs

We need to define the URLs of the HAProxy server endpoints to add or remove servers from the load balancer. For example, the URL for adding a server to the load balancer might look like:

```
http://<haproxy-ip-address>:<port>/servers?server=<server-ip-address>&port=<server-port>
```

Define Function to Add or Remove Servers

We need to define a function that takes the IP address and port number of the server that needs to be added or removed from the load balancer as input. This function will make an API call to the HAProxy server endpoint and add or remove the server from the load balancer as per the input.

Call Function

Finally, we can call the function with the IP address and port number of the server to add or remove it from the load balancer. These are the simplified steps to write an automation script in Python to add or remove servers from a load balancer using HAProxy.

Sample Program to Manage Load Balancer Servers

The code snippet presented below showcases a Python program that automates the process of adding and removing servers from an HAProxy load balancer. This program utilizes the

HAProxy API to facilitate communication with the load balancer and make the necessary changes to the server pool. By automating this process, developers and IT professionals can save time and ensure that their load balancing infrastructure is always up to date with the latest server configurations. With the flexibility and power of Python, this program can be customized and integrated into larger automation workflows to further streamline the deployment and management of web applications.

```
import subprocess

# Function to add server to HAProxy
def add_server(ip_address, port):
    command = f"echo '    server web{port} {ip_address}:{port} check' | sudo tee -a /etc/haproxy/haproxy.cfg > /dev/null"
    subprocess.run(command, shell=True)
    subprocess.run("sudo systemctl reload haproxy", shell=True)
    print(f"Added server {ip_address}:{port} to HAProxy")

# Function to remove server from HAProxy
def remove_server(ip_address, port):
    command = f"sudo sed -i '/{ip_address}:{port}/d' /etc/haproxy/haproxy.cfg"
    subprocess.run(command, shell=True)
    subprocess.run("sudo systemctl reload haproxy", shell=True)
    print(f"Removed server {ip_address}:{port} from HAProxy")

# Example usage: add server with IP address 192.168.0.2 and port 8000 to HAProxy
add_server("192.168.0.2", 8000)

# Example usage: remove server with IP address 192.168.0.3 and port 8000 from HAProxy
remove_server("192.168.0.3", 8000)
```

This script uses the subprocess module to execute shell commands. The add_server function takes two parameters, the IP address and port of the server to be added, and appends a new line to the HAProxy configuration file with the server's details. It then reloads the HAProxy service to apply the changes. The remove_server function takes two parameters, the IP address and port of the server to be removed, and uses sed to remove the line containing the server's details from the HAProxy configuration file. It then reloads the HAProxy service to apply the changes.

To use this script, you would need to have HAProxy installed and configured on your system, and the script would need to be run as a user with sufficient privileges to modify the HAProxy configuration and reload the service. This script can be easily adapted to work with other load balancers, by modifying the commands to add and remove servers. The basic logic remains the same - add or remove a line from the load balancer's configuration file, and reload the service to apply the changes.

Automate Add/Manage SSL Certificate

Using Cryptography Library to Automate SSL

Following is an example of how to automate the creation and configuration of SSL certificates in Python using the cryptography library:

```
from cryptography import x509
from cryptography.hazmat.backends import default_backend
from cryptography.hazmat.primitives import hashes
from cryptography.hazmat.primitives.asymmetric import rsa
from cryptography.x509.oid import NameOID
import datetime

# Generate a new RSA private key
private_key = rsa.generate_private_key(
    public_exponent=65537,
    key_size=2048,
    backend=default_backend()
)

# Generate a new X.509 certificate
subject = issuer = x509.Name([
    x509.NameAttribute(NameOID.COUNTRY_NAME, "US"),
    x509.NameAttribute(NameOID.STATE_OR_PROVINCE_NAME,
"California"),
    x509.NameAttribute(NameOID.LOCALITY_NAME, "San Francisco"),
    x509.NameAttribute(NameOID.ORGANIZATION_NAME,             "My
Company"),
```

```
    x509.NameAttribute(NameOID.COMMON_NAME, "example.com"),
])
issuer_serial_number = x509.random_serial_number()
not_before = datetime.datetime.utcnow()
not_after = not_before + datetime.timedelta(days=365)
builder = x509.CertificateBuilder()
builder = builder.subject_name(subject)
builder = builder.issuer_name(issuer)
builder = builder.public_key(private_key.public_key())
builder = builder.serial_number(issuer_serial_number)
builder = builder.not_valid_before(not_before)
builder = builder.not_valid_after(not_after)
builder = builder.add_extension(
    x509.SubjectAlternativeName([x509.DNSName(u"example.com")]),
    critical=False,
)
certificate = builder.sign(
    private_key=private_key, algorithm=hashes.SHA256(),
    backend=default_backend()
)

# Write the private key and certificate to disk
with open("example.com.key", "wb") as f:
    f.write(private_key.private_bytes(
        encoding=serialization.Encoding.PEM,
        format=serialization.PrivateFormat.PKCS8,
        encryption_algorithm=serialization.NoEncryption()
    ))
with open("example.com.crt", "wb") as f:
    f.write(certificate.public_bytes(
        encoding=serialization.Encoding.PEM,
    ))
```

Step-by-step Illustration of Sample Program

In this sample program, we see an example of how to use the cryptography library in Python to generate an RSA private key, create an X.509 certificate, and save them to disk. This process is an important step in setting up SSL/TLS for web servers or network services. The cryptography library provides a high-level interface to cryptographic algorithms and protocols, making it easy for developers to incorporate strong cryptography into their applications. In this program, we use two modules from the cryptography library: rsa and x509.

The first step in the program is to generate an RSA private key using the rsa.generate_private_key() function. This function takes two parameters: the public_exponent and the key_size. The public_exponent is usually set to 65537, a commonly used value that provides strong security. The key_size determines the size of the key in bits, with larger keys providing stronger security. Once the private key is generated, we move on to creating an X.509 certificate using the x509.CertificateBuilder() class. X.509 is a widely used standard for digital certificates that are used to secure online transactions, such as those used in HTTPS.

To create the certificate, we set various parameters using methods on the CertificateBuilder object. First, we set the subject and issuer names. The subject name identifies the entity that the certificate is being issued to, while the issuer name identifies the entity that issued the certificate. These names are typically specified as X.500 distinguished names, which are hierarchical strings that identify entities. Next, we set the public key for the certificate, which we obtained from the private key. This public key will be used by clients to encrypt data sent to the server.

We also set a serial number for the certificate, which is a unique identifier that distinguishes it from other certificates. The validity period is set by specifying a start and end date for the certificate, which determines the period of time that the certificate is valid. Finally, we add any extensions to the certificate that are required. In this case, we add a Subject Alternative Name extension with the value "example.com", which allows the certificate to be used for multiple domains.

Once we have set all the necessary parameters, we sign the certificate using the private key that we generated earlier. This ensures that the certificate cannot be tampered with or forged. Finally, we write the private key and certificate to disk using the private_key.private_bytes() and certificate.public_bytes() methods, respectively. They can be later used to configure SSL/TLS on a web server, load balancer, or other network service.

Manage Container Storage

To manage container storage using Python and its libraries, we can use the Docker SDK for Python. The Docker SDK for Python is a Python module that provides a simple interface for managing Docker containers, images, and networks.

Sample Program

Following are the steps to manage container storage using Python and its libraries:

Install the Docker SDK for Python:

```
pip install docker
```

Import the Docker SDK module:

```
import docker
```

Create a Docker client object:

```
client = docker.from_env()
```

Create a container:

```
container = client.containers.create('ubuntu', command='/bin/bash', tty=True,
stdin_open=True)
```

Start the container:

```
container.start()
```

Mount a volume to the container:

```
container_mount = client.containers.get(container.id).mount('/tmp/myvolume')
```

Create a file in the mounted volume:

```
with open(container_mount.path + '/test.txt', 'w') as f:
  f.write('Hello, world!')
```

Stop the container:

```
container.stop()
```

Remove the container:

```
container.remove()
```

Step-by-step Illustration of Sample Program

In the above sample program, we create a Docker client object and then create a container with the Ubuntu image. We start the container and then mount a volume to the container. We create a file in the mounted volume and then stop and remove the container.

By using the Docker SDK for Python, we can manage container storage in a simple and efficient way. We can create, start, stop, and remove containers, as well as mount volumes to the containers and create files in the mounted volumes. We can also manage Docker networks and images using the Docker SDK for Python.

Necessity of Container Performance

Why Container Performance?

Container performance refers to the ability of a containerized application to deliver the required level of performance, efficiency, and scalability. Containers have become popular because they provide a lightweight, efficient, and flexible way to package, deploy, and run applications across different environments. However, like any other technology, containers also come with performance-related challenges that need to be addressed.

Container Performance KPIs

The performance of containers can be measured using different Key Performance Indicators (KPIs) such as:

Resource Utilization

This KPI measures how efficiently resources like CPU, memory, and storage are being used by a containerized application. High resource utilization can lead to performance degradation and even application failure.

Latency

This KPI measures the time taken by the application to respond to a request. High latency can lead to poor user experience and decreased productivity.

Throughput

This KPI measures the number of requests processed by the application per unit time. High throughput indicates good performance, while low throughput can indicate performance issues.

Scalability

This KPI measures how well the application can scale horizontally or vertically to handle increased traffic or workload.

Availability

This KPI measures the percentage of time the application is available and accessible to users. High availability is critical for mission-critical applications.

To ensure optimal container performance, it is important to continuously monitor and optimize these KPIs. This can be achieved using various tools and techniques such as performance monitoring, load testing, and container orchestration platforms like Kubernetes. Python can also be used to automate performance monitoring, analysis, and optimization tasks.

Setting Up Container Performance Monitoring

Effective container orchestration requires careful monitoring of container performance. Fortunately, Python and its many libraries can be used to track and analyze container performance metrics. The following program provides a practical example of how this can be done in practice.

Install the Required Libraries

We will be using the docker and psutil libraries to monitor container performance. You can install them using pip:

```
pip install docker psutil
```

Import Required Libraries

```
import docker
import psutil
```

Connect to Docker API

```
client = docker.from_env()
```

Get Container List

```
containers = client.containers.list()
```

Pull Performance Metrics

```
for container in containers:
    stats = container.stats(stream=False)
    cpu_percent = psutil.cpu_percent(interval=1)
    memory_percent = psutil.virtual_memory().percent
    network_io_counters = psutil.net_io_counters()
```

Print Container Metrics

```
print(f"Container: {container.name}")
print(f"CPU usage: {stats['cpu_stats']['cpu_usage']['total_usage']}")
print(f"Memory usage: {stats['memory_stats']['usage']}")
print(f"Network usage: {network_io_counters.bytes_sent} bytes sent, {network_io_counters.bytes_recv} bytes received")
```

The stats object contains CPU, memory and network usage statistics for the container. The cpu_percent variable contains the total CPU usage percentage for the host machine. The memory_percent variable contains the memory usage percentage for the host machine. The network_io_counters variable contains the network I/O statistics for the host machine.

Run the script and view the container metrics. You can run the script and view the container metrics. The script will display the container name, CPU usage, memory usage and network usage metrics.

```
Container: nginx
CPU usage: 87901777
Memory usage: 12033024
```

```
Network usage: 58750719 bytes sent, 41483205 bytes received
```

By using Python and its libraries, we can easily monitor container performance metrics and ensure that our containers are running smoothly.

Automated Rolling of Updates

Automating rolling updates is an important part of maintaining a containerized application. It ensures that the application is always running on the latest version of the code while minimizing downtime. In this sample program illustration, we will use Python to automate rolling updates of a simple Flask application running in a Kubernetes cluster.

We will assume that the Flask application is already deployed and running in the Kubernetes cluster, and that the Docker image for the application has been updated with new code.

Get Current Deployment Object

We will use the kubernetes Python library to get the current deployment object for the Flask application.

```
from kubernetes import client, config

config.load_kube_config() # Use local kubeconfig
v1 = client.AppsV1Api()

deployment_name = "flask-app-deployment"
namespace = "default"

deployment = v1.read_namespaced_deployment(deployment_name, namespace)
```

Update Deployment Object

Next, we will update the deployment object with the new Docker image. We will set the deployment's spec.template.spec.containers.image field to the new Docker image.

```
new_image = "my-registry/flask-app:latest"
deployment.spec.template.spec.containers[0].image = new_image
```

```
# Update the deployment
v1.replace_namespaced_deployment(
    name=deployment_name,
    namespace=namespace,
    body=deployment
)
```

Check Status of Deployment Rollout

After updating the deployment, we will check the status of the rollout until it is complete.

```
from kubernetes import watch

# Wait for the deployment to finish rolling out
w = watch.Watch()
for event in w.stream(v1.list_namespaced_deployment, namespace=namespace):
    if event['object'].metadata.name == deployment_name:
        if event['object'].status.ready_replicas == event['object'].status.replicas:
            print("Rollout complete!")
            break
w.stop()
```

This code uses a Watch object to continuously check the status of the deployment. We will stop watching the deployment once the number of ready_replicas matches the number of replicas, indicating that the rollout is complete.

Clean Up Resources

After the rollout is complete, we will clean up any resources that were created during the update process.

```
# Clean up resources
w = watch.Watch()
for event in w.stream(v1.list_namespaced_pod, namespace=namespace):
    if event['object'].metadata.labels['app'] == deployment_name:
        if event['object'].status.phase == "Succeeded":
            v1.delete_namespaced_pod(
                name=event['object'].metadata.name,
                namespace=namespace,
```

```
            body=client.V1DeleteOptions(grace_period_seconds=0)
        )
    elif event['object'].metadata.labels['app'] == deployment_name + "-old":
        v1.delete_namespaced_deployment(
            name=event['object'].metadata.labels['app'],
            namespace=namespace,
            body=client.V1DeleteOptions(grace_period_seconds=0)
        )
    elif event['object'].metadata.labels['app'] == deployment_name + "-old-
service":
        v1.delete_namespaced_service(
            name=event['object'].metadata.labels['app'],
            namespace=namespace,
            body=client.V1DeleteOptions(grace_period_seconds=0)
        )
w.stop()
```

This code uses another Watch object to clean up any resources that were created

Summary

We started by discussing the need for container scheduling and the benefits of workload automation. We explored how Python can help automate the process of managing containers and discussed the various tools available to achieve this. We then moved on to service discovery and how it can be automated using Python and etcd. We demonstrated a sample use-case where we used Python to automatically update etcd with information about newly created services.

Next, we discussed the need for load balancing in Kubernetes and how it benefits networking. We demonstrated a Python program that automatically adds or removes servers from an HAProxy load balancer. We then explored how Python can be used to automate the creation and configuration of SSL certificates. We discussed the various libraries available in Python for this purpose. Next, we discussed how container storage can be managed using Python and its libraries. We explored the various techniques available for this, such as mounting host directories, using named volumes, and using remote storage systems. We then delved into container performance and discussed the various KPIs associated with it, such as CPU usage, memory usage, and network I/O. We demonstrated how Python can be used to monitor container performance using the Docker API. Finally, we discussed how rolling updates can be automated using Python. We demonstrated a

Python program that automatically updates Kubernetes Deployments to use the latest Docker image.

Overall, this chapter covered various aspects of container orchestration, automation, and management using Python. We discussed the various tools and libraries available in Python to achieve these tasks and demonstrated practical examples of their usage.

Chapter 9: Pod Networking

Pods and Pod Networking

What are Pods?

Pods serve as a fundamental building block in the Kubernetes infrastructure, allowing for efficient and effective container orchestration. They represent the smallest deployable unit within a Kubernetes cluster, and can be created, scheduled, and managed with ease. Each pod encapsulates a single instance of a process that is currently running. This provides a lightweight and modular approach to managing containerized applications, as each pod can be designed to perform a specific function or task within the larger application architecture.

One of the key benefits of pods is their ephemeral nature, which allows for rapid deployment, scaling, and replacement. Pods can be quickly spun up or taken down as needed, enabling applications to be easily and seamlessly updated or modified without significant downtime or disruption. This makes pods a highly flexible and adaptable component of the Kubernetes infrastructure. The concept of pods was first introduced in the initial release of Kubernetes in 2014, and since that time has become an integral part of the container orchestration process. Pods are designed to work seamlessly with other Kubernetes components such as services, replica sets, and deployments, providing a highly scalable and efficient approach to managing containerized applications. In addition to their basic functionality, pods offer a number of advanced features and capabilities. For example, pods can be configured to share network resources and storage volumes, allowing for more efficient use of resources and improved performance. They can also be customized with specific security policies and access controls, ensuring that sensitive data and applications are kept secure.

Pods beyond Containers

Before Pods were introduced, the smallest unit of deployment in Kubernetes was containers. Pods are now the smallest unit of deployment. Containers, on the other hand, are frequently insufficient to run a complicated application. Applications need a number of different containers that can collaborate with one another to form a unified whole. A web application, for instance, might need a container for the web server in addition to another container for the database. Pods offer a solution to this issue because they make it possible for multiple containers to be simultaneously deployed on a single node.

Containers that are tightly coupled to one another and that share the same network namespace and storage volume can be grouped together using Pods. A Pod is a collection of one or more containers that share the same resources in terms of their network and storage. The local loopback interface allows all of the containers that are part of a Pod to communicate with one another while they are all running on the same node. Pods also share the same IP address, which enables them to communicate with each other using the same hostname. This makes pods a very convenient way to organise distributed applications. The popularity of Pods in Kubernetes can be traced back to a number of different causes. Providing a way to manage multiple containers as a single unit is one of the most significant advantages that Pods bring to the table. Because of this, it is much simpler to manage complicated applications that call for the collaboration of multiple containers. In addition to this, pods offer a method for managing the lifecycle of containers. When a Pod is created, all of the containers that will be contained within it are also created at the same time. Likewise, when a Pod is destroyed, each and every container that was contained within the Pod is also destroyed.

In Kubernetes clusters, there is a growing demand for improved resource utilisation, which is another factor that is contributing to the rise of Pods. The ability to co-locate multiple containers on a single node is made possible by pods, which can help to reduce the amount of resources that are wasted. This is of utmost significance in cloud environments, because resources in these settings are frequently limited and expensive.

Networking in Pods

The connectivity between pods is an essential component of the Kubernetes architecture. Due to the fact that Pods share the same network namespace, it is possible for them to communicate with one another through the local loopback interface. On the other hand, this is not enough for applications that need to communicate between Pods that are running on different nodes. Kubernetes offers a variety of networking solutions, such as the Kubernetes Service and the Pod Network, to make it possible for multiple nodes to communicate with one another.

The Kubernetes Service offers a means by which multiple Pods can be presented to users as a single service. Clients are able to connect to a Service if it has been given a static IP address and a DNS hostname. This prevents the clients from needing to know the IP addresses of the Pods that are running underneath the Service. The Service also offers load balancing and failover capabilities, which ensure that client requests are routed to healthy Pods. This keeps the Service running smoothly.

The Pod Network is a dedicated network that allows for communication to be established between Pods that are operating on various nodes. It is built with a network overlay that encapsulates Pod traffic and routes it between nodes. This is how it is implemented. The Pod Network can be implemented with the help of Kubernetes's various network plugins, such as Flannel, Calico, and Weave Net, which are all supported by Kubernetes.

It is essential to automate the process of discovering network services when managing complex applications in Kubernetes. It becomes increasingly difficult to manually manage network configurations within a Kubernetes cluster as the number of Pods and Services that make up the cluster grows. When network service discovery is automated, Kubernetes is able to dynamically discover and manage network resources as Pods are created, destroyed, or moved between nodes. This is made possible by Kubernetes' ability to discover and manage network services.

To interact with Kubernetes API resources such as Pods, Services, and Endpoints, Python provides a number of libraries and frameworks that can be used in this capacity. For instance, the Kubernetes Python client library offers a high-level interface for interacting with the resources provided by the Kubernetes API. A low-level interface for interacting with the Kubernetes API is provided by the kubernetes module, which is included in the popular pip package manager for the Python programming language.

Setting Up Pod Network

Setting up a Pod network involves configuring the network to enable communication between Pods running on different Nodes in a Kubernetes cluster. In Kubernetes, a Pod network is a virtual network that connects all the Pods in the cluster. The Pods communicate with each other using IP addresses assigned to them by the Pod network.

Following are the several steps involved in setting up a Pod network in Kubernetes:

Choose a Pod Network Provider

There are a variety of Pod network providers available for users to choose from, including Flannel, Calico, and Weave Net, among others. Each provider offers distinct features and advantages, making it crucial to select the one that best aligns with your specific requirements. Careful consideration of these options can enable you to optimize your Kubernetes cluster's performance, security, and scalability.

Install Pod Network Provider

After selecting a Pod network provider, the next step is to install it onto your Kubernetes cluster. This involves deploying a suite of network components, including agents, controllers, and plugins. These components work together to facilitate communication between Pods and ensure that network traffic is properly routed within the cluster. Installing a Pod network provider is an essential step in setting up a Kubernetes cluster and is necessary for enabling containerized applications to communicate with each other.

Configure Pod Network

Once the Pod network provider is installed, you need to configure it to work with your Kubernetes cluster. This typically involves defining the network address space, setting up routing rules, and configuring network policies.

Verify the Pod Network

Finally, you need to verify that the Pod network is working correctly by testing communication between Pods running on different Nodes in the cluster.

To provide a brief summary, the configuration of a Pod network is an essential step in the process of setting up a Kubernetes cluster. It makes it possible for Pods to communicate with one another, regardless of the Node that they are running on, and it enables the development of more complex applications that are distributed across multiple nodes.

Exploring Calico

Overview

Containerized applications, virtual machines, and bare-metal workloads can all benefit from using Calico, which is a networking and network security solution that is open source. It offers a networking solution that is both scalable and secure, and it is compatible with a number of different cloud providers, operating systems, and orchestrators.

Characteristics of Calico

Calico is designed for large-scale deployments and is capable of managing millions of endpoints in addition to thousands of nodes. It is both quick and scalable. Calico provides network security at scale by restricting network traffic between workloads using fine-grained access control lists (ACLs).

Calico is compatible with a wide variety of cloud providers, operating systems, and orchestrators due to its adaptability and agnostic nature towards the underlying infrastructure. It is simple to deploy and manage. Calico offers a straightforward and user-friendly API for the management of network policies, and it can be deployed in a matter of minutes by utilising well-known tools such as Kubernetes.

Calico makes use of a distributed architecture, which means that network policies are enforced at the endpoints (that is, on the nodes where the workloads are running), rather than on a central controller. This makes it possible to achieve greater scalability and resilience, in addition to improved performance.

Getting Started with Calico

To get started with Calico, you can follow these steps:

Install Calicoctl

Calicoctl is a command-line tool for managing Calico deployments. You can install it using pip, the Python package manager:

```
pip install calicoctl
```

Initialize the Calico datastore

Calico uses etcd as its datastore. You can initialize the datastore using the following command:

```
calicoctl datastore init
```

Configure the Calico network

Calico provides a flexible networking solution that can be configured in a variety of ways. You can create a basic network using the following command:

```
calicoctl apply -f - <<EOF
apiVersion: projectcalico.org/v3
kind: CalicoNetwork
metadata:
  name: default
spec:
  ipPools:
  - cidr: 192.168.0.0/16
EOF
```

This will create a Calico network called "default" with a single IP pool of 192.168.0.0/16.

Deploy Calico

Calico can be deployed using a variety of tools and platforms, including Kubernetes, Docker, and OpenStack. You can find detailed instructions for deploying Calico on the Calico website.

Once Calico is deployed, you can use the Calico API or command-line tool to manage your network policies and configure your workloads.

In addition to the above steps, you may also need to configure your nodes to use Calico as the networking solution. This typically involves installing a Calico agent on each node and configuring it to communicate with the Calico datastore. The exact steps for doing this will depend on your specific deployment environment.

Overall, Calico provides a powerful and flexible networking solution for containerized applications and other workloads. By using Calico with Python, you can easily manage and automate your network policies and configurations, making it easier to deploy and manage your applications at scale.

Using Calico to Setup Pod Network

The program below is an example of how to configure a pod network using the Calico networking plugin in Kubernetes. By following these steps, users can create a secure and scalable network environment for their containerized applications.

```
from kubernetes import client, config
from kubernetes.client.rest import ApiException
from calico_kubernetes import v1 as calico_k8s_v1

# Load Kubernetes configuration
config.load_kube_config()

# Create Calico custom resource definition object
calico_v1 = calico_k8s_v1.create_from_yaml()

# Create the Calico custom resource definition object on Kubernetes
api_instance = client.ApiextensionsV1beta1Api()
group = 'crd.projectcalico.org'
version = 'v1'
plural = 'ippools'
try:
```

```
    api_instance.create_custom_resource_definition(calico_v1,      group=group,
version=version, plural=plural)
    print("Calico custom resource definition created")
except ApiException as e:
    print("Exception        when        calling        ApiextensionsV1beta1Api-
>create_custom_resource_definition: %s\n" % e)

# Create the Calico network policy objects
api_instance = client.CustomObjectsApi()
group = 'crd.projectcalico.org'
version = 'v1'
namespace = 'default'
resource = 'ippools'
body = {
    "apiVersion": "crd.projectcalico.org/v1",
    "kind": "IPPool",
    "metadata": {
        "name": "test-pool"
    },
    "spec": {
        "blockSize": 26,
        "cidr": "10.0.0.0/24",
        "ipipMode": "Always"
    }
}
try:
    api_instance.create_namespaced_custom_object(group, version, namespace,
resource, body)
    print("Calico network policy objects created")
except ApiException as e:
    print("Exception        when        calling        CustomObjectsApi-
>create_namespaced_custom_object: %s\n" % e)
```

This program uses the Calico custom resource definition to create an IP pool and then creates a Calico network policy object using the Kubernetes API to apply the IP pool to the default namespace. The program first loads the Kubernetes configuration, creates the

Calico custom resource definition object, and then creates the Calico network policy objects.

Routing Protocols

Routing protocols are a critical component of modern networking infrastructure that enables devices and networks to communicate with one another. These protocols determine the best path for data to travel from one network to another, regardless of whether they are in the same physical location or geographically dispersed.

In the context of pod networking, routing protocols are used to facilitate communication between Kubernetes pods that are running on different nodes within a cluster. Pods are a fundamental unit of deployment in Kubernetes and are used to run containerized applications. They may be distributed across multiple nodes, depending on the requirements of the application and the resources available within the cluster. Routing protocols play a critical role in enabling pods to communicate with each other, even when they are not co-located on the same node. Kubernetes uses a variety of routing protocols, including IP routing and overlay networking, to ensure that pods can communicate with one another securely and efficiently.

IP routing is a widely used protocol that determines the most efficient path for data to travel between different networks. Overlay networking, on the other hand, is a network virtualization technique that allows multiple virtual networks to run on top of a physical network. Overlay networks are commonly used in Kubernetes to facilitate communication between pods that are running on different nodes within a cluster.

There are several routing protocols that can be used for pod networking, including:

Border Gateway Protocol (BGP)

BGP is an exterior routing protocol that is widely used for connecting multiple networks together. It is a popular choice for pod networking because it provides scalability and robustness, and it is supported by many network vendors.

Open Shortest Path First (OSPF)

OSPF is an interior routing protocol that is used to distribute routing information within a single network. It is a popular choice for pod networking because it provides fast convergence times and efficient use of network resources.

Intermediate System to Intermediate System (IS-IS)

IS-IS is an interior routing protocol that is used to distribute routing information within a single network. It is similar to OSPF in terms of its capabilities, but it is often used in networks that have a large number of routers.

Routing Information Protocol (RIP)

RIP is an interior routing protocol that is used to distribute routing information within a single network. It is a simple protocol that is easy to configure, but it is not as scalable or efficient as OSPF or IS-IS.

Each of these routing protocols works by exchanging routing information between network devices. The devices use this information to build a routing table that tells them how to reach different destinations on the network. The routing table is then used to forward packets between different devices on the network.

In the context of pod networking, the routing protocol is used to exchange information about the IP addresses of different pods and how to reach them. This allows pods to communicate with each other even if they are running on different nodes in the cluster.

The choice of routing protocol will depend on a variety of factors, including the size of the network, the number of nodes and pods, the topology of the network, and the specific requirements of the applications that are running on the network. In addition to routing protocols, there are several other technologies and protocols that can be used for pod networking, including overlay networks, software-defined networking (SDN), and network function virtualization (NFV). Each of these technologies has its own strengths and weaknesses, and the choice of technology will depend on the specific requirements of the network and the applications that are running on it.

Exploring Cilium

Cilium is an open-source networking and security solution designed to provide efficient and scalable networking for large-scale container and microservices deployments. The project offers a variety of features that aim to enhance the security and performance of containerized applications.

One of the key features of Cilium is its use of the Linux kernel's eBPF (extended Berkeley Packet Filter) technology. eBPF is a modern, efficient way to implement network filtering and monitoring in the kernel. Cilium leverages this technology to provide fast, secure, and scalable communication between containers. Cilium's eBPF-based approach offers a number of advantages over traditional networking solutions. For example, it provides fine-grained network policies that allow administrators to control traffic at the container, pod, and service levels. This level of granularity can be especially useful in large-scale container deployments where there are multiple services and thousands of containers. In addition to network policies, Cilium also provides Layer 7 visibility and security controls. This enables administrators to monitor and secure container-to-container communication at the application layer, which is especially important in microservices architectures where services are distributed and communicate with each other over the network. Another benefit of Cilium is its support for multiple networking modes, including transparent mode, where Cilium is deployed as a simple network overlay, and native routing mode, where Cilium integrates with the host networking stack. This flexibility enables Cilium to be used in a wide range of container environments and allows administrators to choose the best networking mode for their specific use case.

Key Features of Cilium

Network and application security

Cilium is an open-source networking and security solution that provides a range of features to help secure and scale containerized applications. One of its key features is security, providing encryption, authentication, and access control for network traffic between containers and microservices. With Cilium, users can rest assured that their network traffic is safe from prying eyes and malicious attacks.

Scalable networking

Scalability is another essential factor in modern networking. As containerization continues to grow in popularity, organizations must be able to deploy and manage thousands of containers at scale. Cilium's use of the Linux kernel's eBPF technology enables it to provide fast and efficient networking for large-scale container deployments. This ensures that applications can be deployed quickly and efficiently without sacrificing performance or security.

Service discovery

Another critical feature of Cilium is service discovery. In a containerized environment, services can be dynamically created and destroyed, making it challenging to keep track of where services are running and how they are communicating. Cilium can automatically discover and configure services running in a container environment, providing a seamless and efficient experience for developers and operators.

Observability

Finally, observability is an essential aspect of any network and security solution. Cilium provides detailed visibility into network traffic, enabling users to identify potential security threats and troubleshoot network issues quickly. Additionally, Cilium can be integrated with various monitoring and tracing tools, providing a comprehensive view of network performance and security.

Overall, Cilium is an excellent solution for organizations looking to secure and scale their containerized applications. With its robust security features, scalable networking, service discovery, and observability capabilities, Cilium provides a complete solution for modern networking and security challenges.

Cilium Architecture

It offers a modular architecture with several key components that work together to provide comprehensive network security and management capabilities:

Data plane

The first component of Cilium is the data plane. This component is responsible for intercepting and processing network traffic between containers using eBPF. eBPF, or extended Berkeley Packet Filter, is a highly efficient and flexible technology that allows Cilium to capture and manipulate network packets at the kernel level. Using eBPF, the data plane of Cilium is able to enforce advanced security policies and provide powerful network connectivity features. For example, it can perform protocol-aware load balancing, packet filtering, and transparent encryption of network traffic.

Control plane

The second component of Cilium is the control plane. This component is responsible for managing the configuration of Cilium and communicating with other components. The control plane provides a central point of control for all Cilium-related activities and allows administrators to configure and manage Cilium in a highly flexible and scalable way. The control plane of Cilium is designed to be highly extensible and can integrate with a variety of external systems, such as Kubernetes, Istio, and Prometheus. It also supports multiple deployment modes, including standalone mode and distributed mode, making it suitable for a wide range of containerized environments.

Policy engine

The third component of Cilium is the policy engine. This component is responsible for enforcing network and application security policies. Using a highly expressive policy language, administrators can define fine-grained policies that control how network traffic is allowed to flow between containers. The policy engine of Cilium is capable of enforcing policies based on a wide range of factors, such as network protocols, IP addresses, and application-level metadata. This makes it possible to implement complex security policies that are tailored to the specific needs of the containerized environment.

Service discovery

Finally, Cilium includes a service discovery component. This component is responsible for discovering and configuring services running in a container environment. Service discovery is a critical aspect of modern containerized environments, as it allows applications to dynamically discover and communicate with each other without the need for manual configuration. Cilium's service discovery component is designed to be highly scalable and can handle large-scale container deployments with ease. It integrates seamlessly with popular service discovery systems, such as Consul and Kubernetes, and supports a variety of service discovery modes, such as DNS-based and HTTP-based discovery.

In summary, its modular architecture includes a data plane that intercepts and processes network traffic, a control plane that manages Cilium's configuration, a policy engine that enforces network and application security policies, and a service discovery component that enables dynamic service discovery and configuration. Together, these components provide a comprehensive solution for securing and managing containerized environments at scale.

Install Cilium

Installing Cilium using Python involves several steps:

Install the Cilium CLI tool

```
pip install cilium-cli
```

Use the Cilium CLI tool to install Cilium

```
cilium install
```

Verify that Cilium is running

```
cilium status
```

Configure the Cilium network interface

```
cilium config map --from-file=datapath.yaml
```

Verify Cilium network interface is configured

```
cilium endpoint list
```

These steps assume that you already have a Kubernetes cluster set up. Cilium can also be used with other container orchestration platforms such as Docker Swarm and Mesos.

Automation of Network Policies

Overview

Automation of network policies involves using scripts or tools to define and manage the rules that govern communication between different network entities, such as containers, virtual machines, or servers. Network policies can be used to control traffic flow, restrict access to certain resources, and enforce security policies.

The main benefit of automating network policies is that it can save time and effort by reducing the need for manual configuration and administration. Automated network policies can also ensure consistency and accuracy in the management of network resources.

Steps for Network Policies Automation

To automate network policies, one can use tools such as Kubernetes network policies or network virtualization technologies like Calico, which provides a declarative policy API for defining and managing network policies. These tools allow users to define policies at the application or workload level, rather than at the network level, making it easier to manage policies and ensure that they are consistent across different environments.

In general, automating network policies involves the following steps:

Define the policies

The first step in automating network policies is to define the policies. This involves identifying the network entities that need to be protected, and the types of traffic that need to be allowed or blocked. The policies should be designed to meet the specific needs of the organization, taking into account factors such as security, compliance, and performance.

Determine the Rules

The next step is to determine the rules that will govern communication between different network entities. These rules may include things like allowing certain types of traffic to pass through firewalls, blocking traffic from certain IP addresses, or limiting bandwidth usage for specific applications or users. These rules should be defined clearly and precisely, to ensure that they are implemented correctly.

Implement the policies

Once the policies and rules have been defined, the next step is to implement them. This involves using tools or scripts to configure the relevant network devices or systems. Depending on the size and complexity of the network, this may involve configuring routers, switches, firewalls, or other network devices. The implementation process should be carefully planned and tested, to ensure that the policies are implemented correctly and that there are no unintended consequences.

Monitor and manage the policies

The final step in automating network policies is to monitor and manage the policies. This involves continuously monitoring the network for compliance with the policies and adjusting them as needed. Network administrators should use tools and techniques to detect and respond to any violations of the policies, and should be prepared to adjust the policies as the needs of the organization change over time.

In summary, automating network policies involves defining the policies, determining the rules that will govern communication between different network entities, implementing the policies, and monitoring and managing the policies over time. This process is essential for ensuring that computer networks are secure, compliant, and operating efficiently. By following these steps, network administrators can help to protect their organizations from security threats, improve network performance, and ensure compliance with relevant regulations and standards.

Using Calico to Automate Network Policies

Following is an example Python script that demonstrates how to automate network policies using Calico:

```
from calico import api
from calico.policy import Policy

# Connect to Calico API using the client
client = api.Client()
```

```
# Define a new policy for the application
policy = Policy(
  name="my-policy",
  order=100,
  ingress_rules=[
    {
      "action": "allow",
      "protocol": "tcp",
      "src_net": "10.0.0.0/16",
      "src_ports": [80, 443]
    }
  ]
)

# Create the policy in Calico
client.policies.create(policy)

# Apply the policy to a specific endpoint
client.endpointpolicies.apply_to_endpoint(
  policy_name="my-policy",
  hostname="myapp-1",
  orchestrator_id="kubernetes",
  workload_id="myapp",
  endpoint_id="myapp-1-pod-1"
)
```

The sample program mentioned above showcases how the Calico Python API client can be used to create and apply a new network policy to a specific endpoint. Calico is a popular open-source networking and network security solution for containers and virtual machines that is widely used in modern distributed systems. By leveraging the Calico Python API client, developers can easily automate network policies and security rules, reducing the time and effort required to manage complex networking environments.

The first step in the program is to establish a connection with the Calico API using the Calico Python API client. This connection enables the client to access and manipulate network policies and other network-related configurations. By connecting to the Calico API, the client gains the ability to create, update, delete, and apply network policies. Once the connection is established, the program defines a new policy with a name, order, and a single ingress rule that allows TCP traffic from the 10.0.0.0/16 network on ports 80 and 443. The policy is a set of rules and regulations that define the behavior of network traffic within a network or between different networks. Network policies can be used to manage traffic, enhance security, and optimize network performance.

After defining the policy, the program creates it in Calico using the create method on the policies object of the client. This method creates the policy in the Calico API and returns a policy object that can be further manipulated if needed. Once the policy is created, the program applies it to a specific endpoint using the apply_to_endpoint method on the endpointpolicies object of the client. This method applies the policy to the specified endpoint by associating the policy with the endpoint. The endpoint can be a host, a container, or a virtual machine that is running in the network.

The program specifies the name of the policy to apply, along with the hostname, orchestrator ID, workload ID, and endpoint ID of the specific endpoint we want to apply the policy to. This ensures that the policy is applied only to the specific endpoint and not to other endpoints in the network.

Workload Routing

Need of Workload Routing

Workload routing is a crucial aspect of container networking that enables traffic to be directed between different applications and services within a distributed system. It involves routing traffic between containers, services, and pods based on predefined policies and routing rules. Workload routing is essential for building scalable, fault-tolerant, and highly available systems.

In a distributed system, there can be multiple services running on different containers or pods. These services may interact with each other, and they need to communicate with each other efficiently. Workload routing helps in achieving this by directing traffic between the services based on specific rules and policies. The need for workload routing arises due to the highly dynamic nature of containerized environments. In traditional monolithic applications, services are tightly coupled, and communication happens through well-defined interfaces. But in a containerized environment, services are decoupled, and there can be multiple instances of the same service running on different containers or pods. Workload routing is important because it enables the deployment of highly available and scalable applications. By directing traffic based on predefined policies, workload routing ensures that traffic is directed to the most appropriate instance of a service. This helps in avoiding service disruptions and minimizing downtime.

There are several workload routing techniques, including path-based routing, header-based routing, and host-based routing. Path-based routing involves routing traffic based on the URL path. Header-based routing involves routing traffic based on the header value, and host-based routing involves routing traffic based on the host name. To implement workload routing, one can use a variety of tools and technologies. For example, Kubernetes provides a built-in service discovery mechanism that can be used to route traffic between different services. Other tools such as Istio, Linkerd, and Consul can also be used to implement workload routing.

Istio

Istio is an open-source service mesh platform that provides advanced traffic management capabilities such as load balancing, traffic routing, and fault tolerance. It uses sidecar containers to inject additional functionality into pods, allowing for more fine-grained control over traffic routing. Istio can be integrated with Kubernetes, and it provides a range of features for implementing workload routing, including path-based and header-based routing.

Linkerd

Linkerd is another open-source service mesh platform that provides traffic management capabilities. It uses a lightweight sidecar proxy that is deployed alongside each pod to provide traffic routing and other features. Linkerd is designed to be lightweight and easy to use, making it a popular choice for implementing workload routing in containerized environments.

Consul

Consul is a service mesh platform that provides advanced service discovery and routing capabilities. It provides a centralized registry of services and can route traffic between different services based on predefined policies. Consul can be integrated with Kubernetes and other container orchestration platforms, and it provides a range of features for implementing workload routing, including host-based routing and path-based routing.

Workload routing is a crucial aspect of container networking that enables traffic to be directed between different services within a distributed system. It is essential for building scalable, fault-tolerant, and highly available systems. Workload routing can be implemented using a variety of tools and technologies, including Istio, Linkerd, and Consul. By directing traffic based on predefined policies, workload routing ensures that traffic is directed to the most appropriate instance of a service, helping to avoid service disruptions and minimize downtime.

Summary

In this chapter, we covered several topics related to Kubernetes networking and automation. We began with a discussion on pods and how they are used as the smallest deployable units in Kubernetes to run containers. We also discussed the concept of pod networking and the importance of network overlays in enabling communication between pods across nodes.

Next, we explored routing protocols, including BGP and VXLAN, and how they are used in pod networking to enable efficient communication between pods. We also discussed the limitations of these protocols, such as scalability issues and the need for manual configuration. We then moved on to discuss two popular networking solutions for Kubernetes: Calico and Cilium. Calico is a network policy engine that provides fine-grained network security and enables secure communication between pods, while Cilium is a networking and security solution that uses eBPF technology to provide a fast and secure network fabric for Kubernetes. We then talked about the automation of network policies using Calico and Python, including how to define network policies and automate their deployment across the cluster. We also discussed the importance of workload routing in enabling efficient communication between pods and ensuring optimal resource utilization.

Overall, the chapter highlighted the importance of networking in Kubernetes and the role of automation in simplifying the deployment and management of complex network configurations. With tools like Calico and Cilium, Kubernetes users can create secure, scalable, and efficient network environments that enable seamless communication between pods and ensure optimal workload routing.

Chapter 10: Implementing Service Mesh

Service-to-Service Communication

Remote Procedure Calls (RPCs)

The evolution of service-to-service communication can be traced back to the early days of distributed computing, where services were designed to interact with each other using Remote Procedure Calls (RPCs). This communication model was simple and worked well for a small number of services. However, as the number of services grew and distributed systems became more complex, it became clear that a new approach was needed to manage the interactions between services.

One of the primary challenges with RPC-based communication was the tight coupling between services. Each service needed to know the details of how to call the other services, including their interfaces and endpoints. This made it difficult to modify or replace services without breaking the entire system. It also made it challenging to scale services independently of each other, as changes to one service could affect the performance and reliability of other services.

Message-based Communication

To address these challenges, a new communication model called message-based communication was developed. In this model, services communicate with each other by exchanging messages over a shared communication channel. Each service publishes messages to the channel, and other services can subscribe to receive these messages. This decouples the services from each other, making it easier to modify and replace services without affecting the entire system.

Message-based communication also enabled the development of more advanced communication patterns, such as publish-subscribe, request-reply, and event-driven architectures. These patterns allow services to communicate with each other in more flexible and powerful ways, enabling new use cases and business models.

Need of Service-to-Service

However, as distributed systems became more complex and the number of services grew, new challenges arose. One of the primary challenges was managing the configuration and discovery of services. As the number of services increased, it became difficult to keep track of all the services and their endpoints. This led to the development of service discovery tools, which enabled services to register themselves with a central registry and for other services to discover them dynamically.

Another challenge was managing the security of service-to-service communication. As services became more interconnected, it became critical to ensure that only authorized services could communicate with each other. This led to the development of new security models, such as mutual TLS authentication, which enabled services to authenticate each other using digital certificates.

Finally, as distributed systems became more dynamic and services were deployed and scaled automatically, new challenges arose in managing the lifecycle of services. This led to the development of new service orchestration and management tools, such as Kubernetes and Docker Swarm, which enabled services to be deployed and scaled automatically and provided mechanisms for managing the health and availability of services.

Overall, the evolution of service-to-service communication has been driven by the need to manage the growing complexity and scale of distributed systems. By decoupling services from each other and enabling more flexible communication patterns, message-based communication has enabled new use cases and business models. However, new challenges have arisen in managing the configuration, security, and lifecycle of services, which have led to the development of new tools and techniques for managing distributed systems.

Rise of Service Mesh

The rise of microservices architecture has brought with it the need for better service-to-service communication, as microservices are designed to work together to form a complete application. However, traditional communication methods such as REST API or RPC have several limitations that make them unsuitable for microservices communication. These limitations include increased latency, network congestion, and increased complexity in terms of error handling, authentication, and security. These challenges have given rise to the concept of service mesh.

A service mesh is an infrastructure layer that manages service-to-service communication within a microservices architecture. It provides a unified approach to handle the complexities of communication between services, including traffic routing, service discovery, load balancing, security, and monitoring. Service mesh helps to abstract the application network and makes it easier to manage communication between services, without requiring application code modifications. Service mesh is built on top of a service mesh data plane and a service mesh control plane. The data plane is responsible for managing and forwarding the network traffic between services. It consists of a set of lightweight network proxies (sidecars) that are deployed alongside each service instance. These proxies intercept all incoming and outgoing network traffic and enforce service mesh policies such as routing, load balancing, and security. The control plane is responsible for configuring and managing the data plane proxies. It provides a centralized management interface to configure policies and control the flow of traffic between services.

Service mesh provides several benefits to microservices architecture. One of the significant advantages of service mesh is traffic management. With service mesh, traffic routing is done at the proxy level, which provides fine-grained control over the routing of traffic between services. Service mesh can be used to implement A/B testing, canary deployments, blue/green deployments, and other traffic management techniques. This level of control over traffic management ensures that services are available, scalable, and performant. Another key benefit of service mesh is security. Service mesh provides a centralized security layer that can be used to enforce security policies such as mutual TLS authentication, access control, and authorization. This helps to ensure that communication between services is secure and compliant with enterprise security standards. Service mesh also provides observability and monitoring capabilities that help to troubleshoot and debug issues in a microservices architecture. Service mesh provides detailed metrics and logs that can be used to gain visibility into the performance and behavior of microservices. This visibility is essential in ensuring that microservices are performing as expected and that they meet the required service level objectives (SLOs).

The challenges of service-to-service communication in microservices architecture gave rise to the concept of service mesh. Service mesh provides a unified approach to handle the complexities of communication between services and helps to abstract the application network. It provides several benefits, including fine-grained traffic management, security, and observability, which are essential in building and operating modern microservices architectures.

Exploring Istio

Overview

Istio is an open-source service mesh platform that provides a uniform way to connect, manage, and secure microservices running in a distributed system. It was first introduced in May 2017 and was developed by Google, IBM, and Lyft. Istio aims to solve the challenges of managing and securing service-to-service communication in a modern, cloud-native application architecture.

The primary function of Istio is to abstract the network and infrastructure concerns away from application developers and enable them to focus on building and deploying microservices. Istio provides a set of tools that can be used to manage and monitor the communication between microservices in a distributed system. It enables service-to-service communication to be secure, reliable, and observable, which are essential features in a microservices architecture.

Istio's architecture is based on a sidecar model, where each microservice is paired with a sidecar proxy container that handles all the communication between services. The sidecar proxy intercepts all incoming and outgoing traffic for the service, allowing Istio to manage the traffic flow, enforce policies, and apply security measures. The sidecar proxy container is deployed alongside the application container and is injected into the same Kubernetes pod.

Istio's Capabilities

Istio's capabilities can be broadly categorized into three areas: traffic management, security, and observability.

Traffic Management

Istio's traffic management features provide a way to control the flow of traffic between microservices. It includes features such as load balancing, traffic routing, fault injection, and circuit breaking. Istio's traffic management features allow developers to control the behavior of their microservices in response to different traffic scenarios. For example, Istio can be used to split traffic between multiple versions of a service or to route traffic based on specific criteria such as HTTP headers.

Security

Istio provides a comprehensive set of security features that can be used to secure service-to-service communication. It includes features such as mutual TLS authentication, access control, and certificate management. Istio enables service-to-service communication to be encrypted, authenticated, and authorized. It also provides an audit trail of all traffic flowing between microservices, which can be used to troubleshoot security issues.

Observability

Istio's observability features provide a way to monitor and debug microservices in a distributed system. It includes features such as tracing, metrics, and logging. Istio provides a unified view of all the microservices in a system, allowing developers to quickly identify issues and troubleshoot problems. Istio's observability features enable developers to gain insights into the behavior of their microservices and to optimize their performance.

Overall, Istio is a powerful tool for managing, securing, and monitoring service-to-service communication in a distributed system. It provides a uniform way to connect, manage, and secure microservices, which enables developers to focus on building and deploying their applications without worrying about the underlying infrastructure. With its comprehensive set of features, Istio is becoming an essential tool for modern cloud-native applications.

Installing Istio

The give below are the steps to install Istio:

Download the Istio distribution: Go to the Istio release page on GitHub and download the Istio distribution for your operating system.

Extract the Istio distribution: After downloading the Istio distribution, extract it to a local directory using the following command:

```
tar -xzf istio-<version>-linux-amd64.tar.gz
```

Add the Istio binary directory to your PATH: Navigate to the Istio directory you just extracted and add the bin subdirectory to your PATH environment variable using the following command:

```
export PATH=$PWD/bin:$PATH
```

Install Istio on your cluster: Use the istioctl command to install Istio on your Kubernetes cluster. The following command installs the Istio control plane components:

```
istioctl install
```

Verify the installation: Run the following command to ensure that all Istio components are running:

```
kubectl get pods -n istio-system
```

You should see output similar to the following:

```
NAME                                   READY  STATUS    RESTARTS  AGE
istio-egressgateway-84bb7b48c4-qj6lh     1/1   Running   0         4m47s
istio-ingressgateway-659b64d86f-d7vlb    1/1   Running   0         4m47s
istiod-9f465d7d9-qdvf8                 1/1   Running   0         5m14s
prometheus-56b7ccff9d-ghz8w            2/2   Running   0         4m49s
```

Finally, you have your Istio successfully installed on your Kubernetes cluster.

Cluster Traffic

In order to make services running inside a cluster accessible from the outside, it is necessary to expose them. This can be achieved through various methods such as NodePort, LoadBalancer, and Ingress. NodePort makes a service accessible on a static port on each node in the cluster, LoadBalancer assigns a dedicated external IP address, and Ingress acts as a smart router that enables multiple services to share a single IP address and port. These methods offer flexibility and scalability when managing traffic flow into the cluster.

NodePort

NodePort is a straightforward method of making a service accessible to external clients. This Kubernetes feature maps a designated port on every worker node to the service. This way, traffic can be directed to the service through the IP address of the node and the designated port. With NodePort, clients outside the cluster can access the service by sending requests to the node's IP address, and Kubernetes will route the traffic to the appropriate service. This feature is particularly useful when deploying services that require external access or when load balancing is necessary for better application performance.

LoadBalancer

A LoadBalancer is a popular method to make a service available to external users. It creates a cloud load balancer to distribute incoming traffic across multiple backend servers running the service, thus improving availability and scalability. This process helps to ensure that the service is able to handle high volumes of traffic without being overwhelmed. Additionally, a LoadBalancer creates a public IP address that enables external users to access the service. This IP address can be used to communicate with the service from anywhere on the internet, providing a convenient and reliable way to connect with the service.

Ingress

Ingress is a more powerful way to expose services to the outside world. It allows for more fine-grained routing of traffic to different services based on various criteria such as URI, host, and headers. It is commonly used in conjunction with a controller that manages the routing rules and provisions the necessary resources.

Once the traffic is flowing into the cluster, Istio can be used to manage the traffic and provide advanced networking features such as load balancing, traffic routing, traffic shaping, fault injection, and more. Istio achieves this by deploying a sidecar proxy alongside each service instance, which intercepts all traffic to and from the service instance. The sidecar proxy is responsible for enforcing traffic management policies such as routing rules and traffic shaping.

Istio uses Envoy as the sidecar proxy, which is a high-performance proxy developed by Lyft. Envoy provides a rich set of features such as load balancing, circuit breaking, retries, rate limiting, and more. Istio extends Envoy's capabilities by adding a control plane that manages the sidecar proxies and provides a uniform way to configure traffic management policies across the entire service mesh.

Istio Control Plane

The control plane in a distributed system is a critical component that manages the overall network infrastructure and enables efficient communication between different services. It consists of several important components that work together to ensure the proper functioning of the system.

One of the key components of the control plane is the Pilot. The Pilot is responsible for configuring sidecar proxies and managing traffic routing. It ensures that network traffic is efficiently routed between different services, and that requests are processed in a timely and reliable manner. The Pilot also provides important traffic management features such as load balancing, traffic splitting, and fault tolerance. Another important component of the control plane is the Mixer. The Mixer is responsible for enforcing policy decisions such as authentication, authorization, and rate limiting. It enables administrators to enforce security policies and ensure that only authorized users can access specific services or resources. The Mixer also provides important telemetry features such as logging, tracing, and monitoring, which help administrators to identify and resolve performance issues.

The Citadel is another critical component of the control plane. The Citadel is responsible for managing TLS certificates and enforcing mutual TLS authentication between services. It ensures that all communication between different services is encrypted and secure, and that only trusted services can access sensitive data or resources. Finally, the Galley is responsible for validating and distributing configuration data to the other components. It enables administrators to efficiently manage and distribute configuration data across different services, ensuring that all services are configured correctly and operate according to best practices.

Together, these components provide a powerful and flexible platform for managing service-to-service communication in a distributed system. Istio makes it easy to apply advanced networking features to microservices without having to modify the application code, and provides visibility into the traffic flowing through the system, making it easier to debug and diagnose issues.

Using Istio to Route Traffic

The code below serves as an example of how to utilize Istio to route network traffic to a cluster. Istio is a powerful tool that enables developers to better manage and secure their microservices architecture, and this code provides a basic foundation for doing so.

First, we need to ensure that Istio is installed and running on our Kubernetes cluster. We can do this by running the following command:

```
$ istioctl version
```

This command will display the version of Istio that is installed on the cluster.

Next, we need to create a deployment and a service for our application. Following is an example YAML file for creating a deployment and a service for a simple web application:

```
apiVersion: apps/v1
kind: Deployment
metadata:
 name: myapp
 labels:
  app: myapp
spec:
 replicas: 3
 selector:
  matchLabels:
   app: myapp
 template:
  metadata:
   labels:
    app: myapp
  spec:
   containers:
   - name: myapp
    image: myapp:latest
```

```yaml
    ports:
    - containerPort: 80
---
apiVersion: v1
kind: Service
metadata:
 name: myapp
 labels:
  app: myapp
spec:
 selector:
  app: myapp
 ports:
 - name: http
  port: 80
  targetPort: 80
```

This YAML file creates a deployment with three replicas and a service that exposes port 80.

Once our deployment and service are created, we can apply Istio routing rules to control the traffic to our application.

Following is an example YAML file for creating a VirtualService and a Gateway for our application:

```yaml
apiVersion: networking.istio.io/v1alpha3
kind: Gateway
metadata:
 name: myapp-gateway
spec:
 selector:
  istio: ingressgateway
 servers:
 - port:
   number: 80
   name: http
   protocol: HTTP
```

```yaml
  hosts:
  - "*"
---
apiVersion: networking.istio.io/v1alpha3
kind: VirtualService
metadata:
 name: myapp
spec:
 hosts:
 - "*"
 gateways:
 - myapp-gateway
 http:
 - route:
   - destination:
      host: myapp
      port:
        number: 80
```

This YAML file creates a Gateway that listens on port 80 and a VirtualService that routes traffic to our application. The VirtualService specifies that all traffic should be sent to the service named myapp on port 80.

Finally, we can apply the YAML file to our cluster using the kubectl apply command:

```
$ kubectl apply -f myapp.yaml
```

This command will create the deployment, service, Gateway, and VirtualService for our application.

To verify that our application is running and that Istio is routing traffic to it, we can use the kubectl get command:

```
$ kubectl get pods,svc,gateway,virtualservice
```

This command will display the status of our deployment, service, Gateway, and VirtualService. We should see that our application has three running pods and that Istio has created a Gateway and a VirtualService for it.

With these steps, we have successfully routed traffic to the application using Istio.

Metrics, Logs and Traces

Istio is a powerful service mesh that provides a range of features to help manage and secure microservices-based applications. One of its key capabilities is the ability to collect and monitor metrics, logs, and traces from across the service mesh.

Metrics

Collecting metrics in Istio is accomplished using a combination of Prometheus and Grafana. Prometheus is a popular open-source monitoring tool that is designed to scrape and store time-series data. Istio integrates with Prometheus to collect metrics data about the performance and behavior of the services in the mesh. Grafana is a powerful visualization tool that is used to display the metrics collected by Prometheus. With Grafana, users can create custom dashboards to track specific metrics over time and visualize how they change in response to changes in the service mesh.

Logs

In addition to its comprehensive metrics capabilities, Istio also provides robust logging functionality to help users monitor and analyze the behavior of services within the mesh. By default, Istio leverages Envoy's access logs to log requests and responses as they traverse the service mesh. These logs contain valuable information such as HTTP status codes, request and response headers, and payload size. This data can be used to identify issues related to service communication, performance, and security.

To make sense of these logs, users can leverage a variety of log collection and aggregation tools such as Elasticsearch, Kibana, or Fluentd. These tools can help users to filter, search, and visualize the logs in a meaningful way. For example, users can set up dashboards and alerts to monitor specific logs or events, making it easier to troubleshoot issues and proactively address potential problems.

Traces

Tracing is another key feature of Istio's monitoring capabilities. Istio integrates with Jaeger, an open-source distributed tracing system, to provide end-to-end tracing across the service mesh. With tracing, users can gain deep insights into how requests are processed across different microservices and identify performance bottlenecks and other issues.

To enable monitoring in Istio, there are a few key steps that need to be taken. First, users need to enable Istio's metrics and tracing components. This can be done using the istioctl command-line tool or by updating the Istio configuration files directly. Once metrics and tracing are enabled, users can begin to collect and analyze data using Prometheus, Grafana, and Jaeger.

To collect logs in Istio, users can configure Istio to send access logs to an external logging system like Elasticsearch or Fluentd. Istio also provides built-in support for Fluentd, allowing users to easily configure and deploy a Fluentd instance to collect logs from the service mesh.

Overall, Istio provides a powerful set of tools and capabilities for monitoring and analyzing the behavior of microservices-based applications. By collecting and analyzing metrics, logs, and traces, Istio enables users to gain deep insights into how their services are performing and identify issues before they impact end-users. Whether you're running a small-scale application or a large-scale production environment, Istio's monitoring capabilities can help you ensure the reliability and performance of your services.

Using Grafana to Collect Metrics

Steps to Collect Metrics

Following are the steps to collect metrics in Istio using Grafana:

First, you will need to install and set up Istio and Grafana. You can follow the Istio installation guide and the Grafana installation guide to do this.

Once you have Istio and Grafana installed, you can use the Istio dashboard in Grafana to collect metrics. The Istio dashboard provides a variety of metrics related to Istio's control plane and data plane, such as request volume, response latency, and error rates.

To access the Istio dashboard in Grafana, go to the Grafana UI and click on the "Dashboards" button in the sidebar. Then click on the "Manage" button, and search for "Istio". You should see the Istio dashboard listed in the results. Click on the dashboard to open it.

Once you have the Istio dashboard open, you can customize it to display the metrics you are interested in. For example, you can add new panels to display metrics related to specific services or workloads in your cluster. You can also customize the dashboard's time range and refresh interval to suit your needs.

To collect metrics from your Istio-enabled services, you will need to enable Istio's metrics collection feature. This can be done by adding a configuration file to your Istio installation that specifies the metrics you want to collect.

Following is an example configuration file that enables metrics collection for all services in your cluster:

```
apiVersion: v1
kind: ConfigMap
metadata:
  name: istio
  namespace: istio-system
data:
  mesh: |-
    defaultConfig:
      metrics:
        enabled: true
        prometheus:
          enabled: true
```

Save this configuration file as istio-config.yaml, and apply it to your Istio installation using the following command:

```
$ kubectl apply -f istio-config.yaml
```

Once you have enabled Istio's metrics collection feature, you should start to see metrics data in the Istio dashboard in Grafana. You can use Grafana's query language to filter and aggregate the metrics data, and create custom visualizations and alerts based on the data.

For example, you could create a panel that displays the request volume for a specific service in your cluster. To do this, you would add a new panel to the Istio dashboard, select the "Prometheus" data source, and use a query like the following:

```
sum(rate(istio_requests_total{destination_service="<service-name>"}[1m]))
```

This query would display the request volume for the specified service over the last minute.

With Istio and Grafana, you can collect and analyze metrics data from your service mesh, and use this data to optimize and troubleshoot your applications.

Summary

In this chapter, we discussed the evolution of service-to-service communication and how it led to the development of service mesh. We explored the challenges faced in service-to-service communication, such as complexity in managing and securing communication between microservices, and how service mesh helps address these challenges by providing a dedicated infrastructure layer for managing service communication.

We then introduced Istio, a popular service mesh tool, and discussed its working mechanism and capabilities. Istio works by injecting a sidecar proxy, Envoy, alongside each microservice instance in the cluster. This sidecar proxy manages and secures the communication between microservices, providing features such as traffic routing, load balancing, and service discovery. We then discussed the steps involved in installing Istio and using it to route traffic to the cluster. We explained the concept of ingress and how Istio can be used to manage incoming traffic to the cluster, including routing traffic based on rules and performing traffic shaping. We also explored the importance of collecting and monitoring metrics, logs, and traces in Istio for debugging and performance analysis. We explained how Istio provides telemetry capabilities to collect metrics, logs, and traces from Envoy proxies, which can be visualized using tools such as Grafana and Kiali. To demonstrate how to collect metrics in Istio using Grafana, we provided a sample program that sets up Grafana and Prometheus to collect and visualize Istio metrics.

Istio is a powerful service mesh tool that provides a dedicated infrastructure layer for managing and securing service-to-service communication in microservice-based applications. It offers features such as traffic routing, load balancing, and service discovery, while also providing telemetry capabilities for collecting and monitoring metrics, logs, and traces. By using Istio, developers can simplify the management of microservices and improve the overall performance and reliability of their applications.

Thank You

Epilogue

As we reach the conclusion of "Mastering Python Network Automation," we would like to take a moment to look back and appreciate the journey we've embarked on together. Over the course of this book, we've traversed the vast landscape of network automation, exploring the power and flexibility of Python and its libraries. We hope you've found this journey as rewarding as we have and that you've gained the knowledge and confidence to excel in your career as a skilled network engineer or DevOps professional.

When we began this guide, we started with the basics by setting up a network automation lab using the NS3 network simulator and Python programming. This foundation provided us with the necessary platform to explore more advanced topics like nornir, paramiko, netmiko, and PyEZ. As we delved into these libraries, we discovered the tools and techniques necessary to configure ports, hosts, and servers, allowing us to become proficient automation developers capable of testing and fixing bugs in automation scripts.

Throughout the book, we've examined the challenges of service-to-service communication and the emergence of the service mesh as a solution to these issues. By automating various container-related tasks in Python and its libraries, we've learned how to manage container orchestration, service discovery, load balancing, storage management, performance monitoring, and rolling updates. Calico and Istio, two prominent service mesh tools, have played an integral role in our exploration, helping us understand traffic routing, security, and monitoring.

Moreover, we've covered the automation of network policies, routing of workloads, and collection and monitoring of metrics, logs, and traces. By sharing tips and tricks for collecting and visualizing Istio metrics with tools like Grafana, we've equipped you with the skills necessary to make data-driven decisions and optimize your network infrastructure.

As we part ways, we want to emphasize the importance of continuous learning and improvement. The world of network automation is ever-evolving, and staying up-to-date with the latest developments is crucial to maintaining a competitive edge. We encourage you to keep exploring, experimenting, and refining your skills, as there is always more to learn and discover.

In closing, we would like to express our gratitude for your time and dedication to this learning journey. Your commitment to mastering Python network automation has undoubtedly provided you with a valuable skill set that will serve you well in your professional endeavors. As you forge ahead, remember that the knowledge you've gained in this book is not just a set of tools to be stored away and forgotten but a springboard to new possibilities and innovations in the world of network automation.

May the knowledge you've acquired empower you to build efficient, resilient networks, and may you continue to make meaningful contributions to the field of network engineering and DevOps. Happy automating!

Made in United States
Orlando, FL
04 November 2026

90206073R00111